COMBAT AIRCRAFT

147 F-4 PHANTOM II *WILD WEASEL* UNITS IN COMBAT

SERIES EDITOR TONY HOLMES

147

COMBAT AIRCRAFT

Peter E Davies

F-4 PHANTOM II *WILD WEASEL* UNITS IN COMBAT

OSPREY

PUBLISHING

OSPREY PUBLISHING

Bloomsbury Publishing Plc

Kemp House, Chawley Park, Cumnor Hill, Oxford, OX2 9PH, UK

29 Earlsfort Terrace, Dublin 2, Ireland

1385 Broadway, 5th Floor, New York, NY 10018, USA

E-mail; info@ospreypublishing.com

www.ospreypublishing.com

OSPREY is a trademark of Osprey Publishing Ltd

First published in Great Britain in 2023

A catalogue record for this book is available from the British Library.

ISBN: PB 9781472854568; eBook 9781472854575; ePDF 9781472854582; XML 9781472854551

23 24 25 26 27   10 9 8 7 6 5 4 3 2 1

Edited by Tony Holmes
Cover Artwork by Gareth Hector
Aircraft Profiles by Jim Laurier
Index by Zoe Ross
Typeset by PDQ Digital Media Solutions, UK
Printed and bound in India by Replika Press Private Ltd

Osprey Publishing supports the Woodland Trust, the UK's leading woodland conservation charity.

To find out more about our authors and books visit **www.ospreypublishing.com**. Here you will find extracts, author interviews, details of forthcoming events and the option to sign up for our newsletter.

Acknowledgements

The author is grateful for the valued assistance of Lt Col Ed Ballanco USAF (ret), Lt Col Bruce Benyshek USAF (ret), Col Kurt Dittmer USAF (ret), Lt Col Stan Goldstein USAF (ret), Lt Col Allen Lamb USAF (ret), Col William Redmond USAF (ret), Capt Ed Sandelius USAF (ret), Col Jim Uken USAF (ret) and other members of the Society of *Wild Weasels*.

Front Cover

F-4G-42-MC 69-0250, callsign 'Coors 36', from the 81st TFS at Sheikh Isa AB, Bahrain, was one of six F-4G *Wild Weasels* participating in Mission 1231W on the opening morning of Operation *Desert Storm* on 17 January 1991. Only two jets, 'Coors 35' and '36', were ready at take-off time to support an attack by Doha-based F-16Cs of the 614th TFS on the Iraqi-occupied airfields at Ali Al Salem and Ahmed al Jaber in Kuwait. 69-0250, crewed by Lt Cols Ed Ballanco (aircraft commander) and Don Whittler (EWO), was flying as wingman to 'Coors 35', crewed by Maj Mark Turberville and Capt Steve Garland. The F-16C formation flew about ten miles ahead of the *Weasels* rather than just behind them.

Approaching the F-16Cs' target area at 28,000 ft and 0.95 Mach, 'Coors 36' picked up several SAM emitters ahead of them. They fired one of four AGM-88 HARMs at the closest site to the target from a range of about 40 miles, and it took around 2.5 minutes to reach its target. A second HARM 'immediately followed this shot' from 'about 35 miles, with about a two-minute time of flight'. The crew of 'Coors 36' then went on to fire their remaining two HARMS, with the final shot taking out a 'Fan Song' radar which had just launched an SA-2 that was closing in on Capt Phil Ruhlman's F-16C. The SAM lost guidance and exploded harmlessly (*Cover artwork by Gareth Hector*)

Previous Pages

A tidy trio of 190th FS Idaho ANG F-4Gs with practice bombs on their wing racks form up for a photograph en route to the range. The only ANG unit to receive F-4Gs (no fewer than 36 *Weasels* were supplied by the 35th and 52nd FWs), the 190th completed its conversion from the RF-4C in the summer of 1991. They were flown until 1996 when the unit began conversion to the C-130, leaving only 'sharkmouthed' F-4G 69-7551, which served in Vietnam (as an F-4E) and in *Desert Storm,* as a gate guardian at the squadron's Gowen Field home (*USAF*)

CONTENTS

CHAPTER ONE

BIRTH OF SEAD

uppression of enemy air defences (SEAD) steadily increased in importance during the wars of the late 20th century to the point where offensive air activity became unfeasible without it. In Operation *Desert Storm* in 1991, SEAD was a vital factor in preventing substantial losses for Coalition air forces, but its origins extended back to the advent of radar in the early 1940s. Britain's Chain Home radar network enabled the Royal Air Force (RAF) to engage the Luftwaffe's numerically superior, escorted bomber formations by giving fighters up to 30 minutes warning to position themselves for effective interceptions. The Germans immediately began targeting the RAF's radar masts once their significance was realised.

During World War 2, basic anti-radar tactics were also developed. Bomber missions were re-routed to avoid known radar sites and Flak positions. Another simple strategy, developed in 1943 and still in use today, involved clouds of tiny metal strips dispensed from aircraft as 'chaff'. Radar beams reflected from the chaff registered potential aircraft formations, while the actual formation was up to 2000 ft away.

The 1940s also saw the genesis of electronic counter measures (ECM), beginning with *Carpet*, the code name for equipment in bombers that emitted radio waves to jam *Würzburg* gun-laying radars. From 1943, 16th Reconnaissance Squadron *Ferret* B-17F Flying Fortress bombers were equipped with APA-24 direction finding units to record radar

A camouflaged SA-2 (or 11D, the standard S-75 export model) on its SM-63-1 launcher near Hanoi in the late 1960s. Difficulty in locating and attacking SAM sites, due to their mobility and camouflage, during their first six months of operations in the Vietnam War brought a new emphasis on defeating them through electronic methods by detecting and jamming their command frequencies (*Dr István Toperczer*) frequencies for subsequent analysis. In the Far East, Ferret-equipped B-29 Superfortresses and B-24 Liberators (known as 'Ravens') detected and analysed Japanese early-warning radars, while heavily-armed A-26 Invaders fitted with APA-24 equipment located and destroyed radar sites. In response to these threats, enemy radar operators turned off their gun-laying radar sets – a tactic which has been a universal defensive response ever since.

Aside from developing radar-guided Flak batteries, German scientists at the Peenemünde research centre had also pioneered the development of the surface-to-air missile (SAM), known as the *Wasserfall*, in 1942. Its technology, captured by Soviet forces in 1945, would eventually give rise in the 1950s to the first ground-to-air missile to see combat in the form of the V-750 Dvina (NATO code-name SA-2 'Guideline'). It had both proximity and impact fuses, and its guidance system employed effective radar control. Dvina and its successors armed the air defence networks of the Soviet Union and its client states, including Iraq, for decades.

During the 1950s, the US emphasis on its nuclear bomber fleet siphoned off funds that might have advanced its SEAD capability. As part of its dominance in acquiring defence funding, Strategic Air Command (SAC) took on the responsibility for suppressing the supposedly limited threat from Soviet air defences by relying on stand-off weapons such as AGM-28 Hound Dog missiles to bypass anti-aircraft artillery (AAA) defences. Tactical Air Command (TAC) was thereby denied adequate funding for SEAD.

Although up to 1000 SA-2 'Guideline' batteries had been established in the USSR from 1957, and its early test launches had been photographed by CIA-operated U-2 reconnaissance aircraft, the missile's lethal power was not encountered by US aircraft until 1 May 1960 when a U-2C flown by Francis Gary Powers was destroyed as it overflew the Soviet Union near Sverdlovsk.

SA-2s were next encountered in Cuba in September 1962 when US electronic intelligence (ELINT) aircraft detected emissions from the P-12 Yenisei ('Spoon Rest') search radars used with the missile. On 27 October three SA-2s from the 507th Anti-aircraft Missile Regiment, situated near Banes, in Cuba, destroyed a U-2F from the 4080th Strategic Reconnaissance Wing, killing pilot Major Rudy Anderson. With 144 Soviet SA-2 launchers, Cuba had suddenly become an extremely hazardous area for US aircraft, which lacked ECM provision. Noise jamming equipment used by SAC's bombers to disrupt hostile radar emissions had been denied to the U-2 Wing in case it fell into enemy hands. The units were too heavy for installation into the U-2s in any case.

In an attempt to solve this issue, the USAF contracted Applied Technology Inc. of Palo Alto, California, to modify an earlier Granger Associates repeater known as System 9 so that it would fool enemy fighter radars with deceptive signals. The repeater was combined with a lightweight radar homing and warning system (RHAW) to show when an aircraft was being tracked by the SA-2's 'Fruit Set' (later, 'Fan Song') radar.

At the same time, the US Navy was equipping its A-3B Skywarrior bombers with Sanders AN/ALQ-49 or AN/ALQ-51 'gate stealers' that would receive a radar pulse, delay it and then return it. An enemy radar then 'saw' the target aircraft at a position several hundred feet from its true location. Hostile radars might also receive multiple returns to deceive a missile or radar-directed gun. Diverting a SAM detonation to 600–800 ft from an aircraft would spare it serious damage.

VIETNAM

Tests with an SA-2, constructed in the USA with data from captured missiles and a 'Guideline' operating manual, enabled tactics experts to devise the most widely used high-g dive-and-turn manoeuvre to evade an oncoming missile if it was seen in time. On 13 February 1966, a Ryan Model 147E drone flying near Hanoi recorded the missile's proximity fuse codes and the radar codes for the downlink and uplink signals to and from the missile that provided data for its guidance by 'Fan Song' operators. In the US Assistant Secretary to the Air Force's opinion, the drone recording was 'the most significant contribution to electronic reconnaissance in the past 20 years'.

From early 1965, North Vietnam's rudimentary AAA defences had been expanded into a fully integrated air defence system comprising radar-directed guns, SA-2 missiles and early-warning radars such as the P-35 'Bar Lock', all supervised by Soviet personnel. Supplies of SA-2s were confined to the basic Almaz-designed SA-75N Dvina, rather than the later, jamming-resistant 13-D Desna or 20D Volkhov versions.

One of the 34.5-ft long missile's major advantages was its mobility. Carried on a PR-11AM transporter-loader towed by a ZiL-151 tractor lorry, an SA-2 could be transferred directly by electric motors onto its SM-63-1 single-rail launcher. All the SA-2 unit components were road transportable, including the Almaz RSNA-75 'Fan Song' radar van, the low frequency, van-mounted P-12 Yenesei 'Spoon Rest' radar and the PRV-11 'Side Net' height-finding radar, preceded in that role by the P-10 'Knife Rest'. Six launchers and 12 missiles were placed on a prepared SAM site, with room to park their transporter-loader supply vehicles. The system's degree of mobility would still be a challenge for *Wild Weasel* Phantom IIs in Operation *Desert Storm* more than 25 years later.

By December 1965 there were 64 prepared SA-2 sites defending Hanoi and Haiphong. Pre-emptive air attacks were ruled out to avoid possible losses of Soviet 'advisors' and an escalation in Moscow's hostile intent. Some American intelligence officials believed that the SAMs would only be used if there was an all-out attack on Hanoi. This wishful thinking was dispelled on 24 June 1965 when Lt Konstantinov Mikhailovich supervised an SA-2 team which shot down a 47th TFS/15th TFW F-4C Phantom II and damaged the remaining three jets in its 'Leopard' flight, 55 miles from Hanoi. The missile had emerged through thick cloud, leaving no time for Capts Richard Keirn and Ross Fobair to out-manoeuvre it.

Like other pilots, they had received no training in SAM avoidance or information about the threat. Like the F-105 Thunderchiefs they were escorting that day, their Phantom II had no electronic protection against enemy radar or missile threats. It was the first US wartime loss to the SA-2, and the subsequent shockwaves in the Pentagon following the jet's destruction energised a purposeful SEAD effort. Air attacks on several

The threat posed by the SA-2. On 12 August 1967 seven miles northeast of Hanoi, Capts Edwin Atterberry and Thomas Parrott of the 11th TRS/432nd TRW were forced to eject from RF-4C 65-0882 after it was hit by a 'Guideline' missile while flying at 18,000 ft on a battle damage assessment mission over a recently bombed bridge. Both men were quickly captured, and Atterberry later died at the hands of North Vietnamese guards after a failed escape attempt in May 1969. Parrott was released at the end of the war (*USAF*)

identified sites proved costly, however, with six Thunderchiefs being lost in three days, mainly to AAA 'flak traps'. According to the USAF's 1973 *Corona Harvest* report, it was now facing 'the most formidable electromagnetic threat ever encountered by US tactical forces'.

With its aircraft also now at risk of being shot down by SAMs, the US Navy took the SEAD lead in Vietnam. It had in fact commenced work on finding a way to defeat the SA-2 shortly after its RF-8 Crusader photo-reconnaissance pilots had been targeted over Cuba in 1962. The US Navy's China Lake Naval Ordnance Test Station introduced the AGM-45A/B Shrike anti-radiation missile (ARM) in 1963, followed by the Melpar AN/APR-23 'Redhead' radar warning receiver in the spring of 1964 in Project Shoehorn, to deal with the SA-2 threat. The Shrike project would produce an ARM that remained in use until the early 1990s, while 'Redhead' displayed range indications on a small 2.5-inch screen showing the intensity of three different sets of radar pulse repetition frequencies, but not their direction.

The Shrike ARM, based on the Raytheon AIM-7 Sparrow III air-to-air missile, was released in a 45-degree loft manoeuvre and climbed in an arc, seeking an emitting target in an area of sky four miles long by one mile wide and then guiding itself to the point of impact. Its small 147-lb blast fragmentation warhead meant the weapon was light enough for carriage by the US Navy's A-4E Skyhawk – its first SEAD platform. However, because of its modest size, the AGM-45 was only capable of damaging a radar antenna.

If the SEAD aircraft was pointed at the threat-emitting radar, the missile was launched ballistically and, when activated, its own radar seeker would detect and lock onto the radar antenna's waves. Later modifications included a white phosphorous charge in the warhead to indicate a hit.

It was also modified for short-range use against radar targets of opportunity, rather than 'lofting' the weapon from its maximum range. By speeding up the guidance process this 'Dive Modified' version began to guide as soon as it was launched, heading straight for the target from a distance of just two to three miles.

Shrike was innovative and had some success, but it was more effective in persuading radar operators to shut down their equipment in response to the threat of an ARM launch. If the 390-lb missile was airborne when a shutdown or change of frequency by the radar target occurred, its monopulse crystal video receiver would break lock and miss the target.

The weapon's short 12-mile range placed the launch aircraft well within the 40-mile range of an N-band 'Fan Song' radar and the 18-mile effective range of the SA-2, which travelled much faster than a Shrike. Attacking from closer range gave the launching aircraft little time to avoid a SAM. The later AGM-45B version, with an Aerojet Mk 78 motor, could achieve a 25-mile range when 'lofted' from medium altitude. It could not be re-programmed in flight to respond to more than one radar frequency (later versions could be switched mid-flight to cover a modest selection of frequencies), while SAM operators could switch between frequency bands to deny the Shrike a target.

US Navy tactics for its *Iron Hand* defence suppression missions, which were mainly flown by A-4s, often required Shrike launchers to 'loft' their missiles towards known radar sites to make them shut down, while other aircraft attacked the sites with bombs, cluster bomb units (CBUs) or Zuni unguided rockets (which could be mistaken for a Shrike by radar operators). Their AN/APR-23 receivers could identify emissions from 'Fan Song' or 'Fire Can' AAA radars as a 'spike' on the display screen that enlarged as the aircraft neared a hostile radar source, although it could not tell whether a radar was just tracking them or was locked onto an aircraft preparatory to a SAM launch. However, from late 1965 onwards *Iron Hand* flights contributed significantly to a declining SA-2 success rate.

USAF *WEASELS*

While the US Navy and US Marine Corps were relatively well-equipped to deal with radar threats in Vietnam, the USAF had devoted meagre funding to tactical SEAD. The Phantom II loss on 25 July 1965 initiated urgent plans to find more effective SAM suppression approaches than hazardous conventional bombing attacks on the sites. Having rejected the AN/APR-23, the USAF turned to external noise-jamming pods under a Quick Reaction Capability (QRC) initiative to find rapid solutions.

Since 1961, Air Force Systems Command had been working on a QRC-160 externally powered pod that could jam both AAA and missile fire control systems and also disrupt search radars in later MiG fighters. The project had been under-resourced until 3 August 1965, when Brig Gen Kenneth Dempster, the dynamic Director of Operational Requirements and Development, re-energised the QRC-160 programme.

Tactical aircraft flying over North Vietnam were soon carrying QRC-160-1A (later, AN/ALQ-71) pods to jam S-, C- and L-band radars, or QRC-160-2 (AN/ALQ-72) for X-band frequencies. Bolted to the

F-100F-21-NA 58-1221 was the first *Wild Weasel* conversion, and the second of the initial batch of modified Super Sabres to be lost when it sustained engine failure on 13 March 1966 over Thailand (*USAF*)

external pylons of F-105 and F-4 fighter-bombers flying in four-aircraft 'pod formations' to maximise the jamming signals, the pods soon became essential for all Operation *Rolling Thunder* attacks on heavily defended areas. Although losses of F-105s were reduced, the pods proved to be ineffective for solo *Wild Weasel* SEAD aircraft attacking SAM sites at close quarters.

Dempster's other main initiative was through proposals for internal ECM equipment to match the AN/APR-23. Based on earlier tests with the QRC-253-2 homing system, which was installed in several F-100F Super Sabres to counter US MIM-23 Hawk SAMs during the extensive 1964 Exercise *Goldfire*, and on new proposals from ATI and Bendix, Dempster initiated Project *Wild Weasel* in August 1965. Four 27th TFW F-100Fs were rapidly equipped with Vector IV (later, AN/APR-25(V) RHAW) equipment and the IR-133 panoramic receiver that would later be developed into the AN/APR-26 launch warning receiver. Three more Shrike-capable conversions were added in February 1966. Their role was the daunting task of locating radar sites for accompanying strike fighters to destroy. Dempster's committee also recommended the development of an air-to-ground anti-radar missile.

ATI's Vector IV, in secret use in some CIA U-2s, was an off-the-shelf system of five boxes that replaced the F-100F's Doppler navigation system and navigation computers. It gave a 360-degree warning of SAM launches, showing the direction and strength of the missile(s), AAA or airborne threats on a small cockpit scope. IR-133 was a separate unit that collected and analysed S-band radar transmissions at longer range, indicating the direction of radar sites.

Electronic warfare officers (EWO), the majority of whom were from SAC bomber units since most tactical aircraft had not previously required such crewmen, occupied the rear cockpits of the F-100Fs. A CRT display showed to within a few degrees whether the radar threat was to the left or right of the aircraft, based on the intensity of two 'spikes' on a screen.

EWOs then 'steered' their pilots, keeping the spikes equal in strength so that the jet was heading towards the threat.

The other vital system, developed in September–October 1965, was the WR-300 (AN/APR-26) launch warning receiver – a tuned crystal that detected SA-2 L-band guidance signals and displayed their intensity, tracking the approach of a missile. It could not show whether the threat was ahead of the aircraft or behind it.

The task of duelling with SA-2s was seen as almost suicidal by some pilots who were approached to join the project. Amongst those in the initial cadre of USAF *Wild Weasel* pilots hand-picked from volunteers were Capts Jack Donovan and Allen Lamb. When told of the role he and Lamb would now be undertaking, Donovan allegedly responded with the comment, 'You gotta be shittin' me!' Lamb described this as 'the natural response of an educated man [a veteran EWO on B-52s] upon learning that he was to fly back-seat to a self-absorbed fighter pilot while acting as flypaper for SAMs'. Although squadronmate Capt Ed Sandelius observed that Donovan said the same thing regarding just about everything, his words became the lasting motto of the *Wild Weasel* community, tastefully abbreviated to 'YGBSM'.

Preparing for the *Weasels'* unprecedented missions in Vietnam was challenging, as Capt Lamb explained;

'There was no training to speak of. It was "cut and paste" to see if it would work. We did run against the SADS [surface-to-air defence system] at Site 7 at Eglin AFB [in Florida] to check the accuracy of the equipment. Then we went to war to see if it would work. Each crew did its own thing.'

The guileful tactics, described by one *Weasel* pilot as 'three-dimensional chess, where cheating is legal', that were soon embedded in *Weasel* procedures also had their origins in these early missions, as Lamb recalled;

'I would offset so that the site didn't think we were homing in on them. Once I had two rings or more on the [IR-133 repeater] scope, I would use the Vector IV to look for the site on the ground, but I would still get readings from the EWO as, in some cases, there was more than one site.'

When a target was firmly established, the F-100F pilot could attack it with 2.75-inch rockets from LAU-3 pods, followed up with bombs and rockets from an *Iron Hand* F-105 flight. The first four F-100Fs arrived at Korat Royal Thai Air Force Base (RTAFB), in Thailand, on 21 November 1965 as the 6234th TFW (*Wild Weasel* Detachment). During the detachment's early missions, the Soviet radar operators simply closed down to avoid detection. Capt Ed Sandelius, as part of the first crew to arrive, told the author that 'We had good ELINT on the SAM sites, but with the ability of the SAM units to pick up and move at short notice, we had to rely on our own equipment'.

The extreme hazards of the F-100F mission soon became apparent when Capts John Pitchford and Bob Trier were shot down on 20 December. Two days later, Capts Lamb and Donovan scored the Detachment's first victory against a SAM site. Homing in on it from their first Vector IV response at a distance of 100 miles, they followed the strobe indications until they 'curled away' to the left and right on the scope, showing that they were above a site. Lamb inverted the jet, reversed and attacked at very low level (most of their missions were flown below an altitude of 500 ft).

Capts Allen Lamb and Jack Donovan step out for another *Wild Weasel* mission at Korat RTAFB in December 1965. Both aviators were part of the initial cadre of USAF *Wild Weasel* pilots who crewed four specially modified F-100Fs assigned to the 6234th TFW (*Wild Weasel* Detachment) (*Lt Col Allen Lamb*)

'My rockets hit short, but as I pulled off there was a bright flash. I must have hit the oxidizer van for the SA-2 liquid fuel motors', Lamb recalled. He radioed the site's location to a nearby flight of F-105s, which quickly joined him in a series of attacking passes that saw 304 rockets and 2900 rounds of 20 mm ammunition expended and the target destroyed.

Another innovation that continued into lasting *Weasel* strategy was the use of a diving turn into the missile's trajectory, breaking away as late as the pilot's nerves could stand, in order to prevent a SAM from correcting its course and exploding close to the aircraft. Multiple F-100Fs were employed per mission, as Lamb explained;

'We had one *Weasel* before the strikers and a second about 20 minutes into the strike, or when the first *Weasel* was at bingo fuel or had expended its ordnance. They would let us troll for radar sites, which was better than being with the strikers.'

By the time of Operation *Desert Storm*, *Weasel* tactics had evolved to usually include additional aircraft to cover the exit of a strike package to prevent it being 'shot in the back'.

The small F-100F Detachment's *Wild Weasel I* work had laid the foundations for a more extensive SEAD operation, and Brig Gen Dempster chose the F-105F Thunderchief as the next *Weasel* aircraft, although the F-4C Phantom II had also been considered. The F-105 was much faster than the F-100F, and unlike the latter, it used the USAF's standard Flying Boom in-flight refuelling system. The Super Sabres remained at Korat until July 1966, making the first USAF combat firing of a Shrike on 18 April when a *Weasel* flown by Majs Don Frazier and Marshall Goldberg claimed a possible 'Fire Can' kill. Half of the original F-100F complement had been lost by the time the detachment returned to the USA, although they had destroyed nine SA-2 sites (three by Capt Lamb's crew) and forced many others to shut down during *Rolling Thunder* operations, thus reducing USAF losses.

CHAPTER TWO

WILD WEASEL II, III AND *IV*

By mid-August 1966 American airmen were facing a fully integrated air defence network in North Vietnam, with interconnected SAM and AAA radars sharing information on the location and heading of incoming aircraft targets. These elements refined the more general information passed to them by long-range early warning radars working in long wavelengths. A year later, the number of 'Fan Song' units in place throughout North Vietnam had increased from 20 (at the time of the first *Wild Weasel I* operations) to 270, and their mobility enabled them to be moved to less populated regions to ambush strike flights. SA-2s had accounted for 110 US aircraft by 1968, with radar-guided AAA downing many more. The USAF's response was formalised in the Tactics Manual of the 388th TFW at Korat;

'The mission of the *Wild Weasel* aircrew generally falls into two roles – *Iron Hand* to suppress and *Wild Weasel* to destroy. Tactics employed on the *Iron Hand* missions are primarily designed to suppress the SA-2 and gun-laying radars of North Vietnam during the ingress, attack and egress of the main strike force. AGM-45 Shrike are used to kill, or at least harass, the SA-2 and/ or "Fire Can" radar transmitters. Coincidentally, the threat represented by the *Iron Hand* flight also diverts the attention of enemy radar operators from the main strike force, and this is also a form of suppression.'

The destruction of enemy air defences, rather than suppression, gradually acquired its own acronym, DEAD, which became a dominant

With its weapons load fully intact, F-105G-1-RE 62-4425 *KLOYJAI* of the 17th WWS/388th TFW returns to Korat RTAFB on 29 December 1972 at the conclusion of the final *Wild Weasel* mission of Operation *Linebacker II*. Capts Jim Boyd and Kim Pepperell obviously found no targets for their Shrike missiles, since North Vietnam's defences had been substantially neutralised by then (*USAF*) aspect of anti-radar operations in the 1990s. Some definitions of SEAD also included destruction of enemy air interception assets.

A replacement aircraft for the F-100F *Wild Weasel II* could have been the F-4C Phantom II, and initial installation trials with the anti-radiation fit began. Unlike the F-105, it was in production, and becoming TAC's standard fighter-bomber and reconnaissance platform. However, those who worked on the project found it beset with problems, including random electrical interference and variations in voltage potential throughout the airframe due to incompatibility between the aircraft's electrical wiring and the new equipment. The project was shelved and the F-105F was selected instead, despite the relatively small total of 143 airframes built for training purposes.

Republic had already successfully tested the AN/APS-107 RHAW in both an F-105D and an F-105F (together with the AN/ALQ-51 antenna and QRC-160-1 jamming pod) in September 1965. This project became *Wild Weasel II*, replaced by *Wild Weasel III* in October 1965. The latter development used the same equipment as the *Wild Weasel I* F-100Fs, and the first installation was complete by 3 February 1966, with six more in progress. After competitive tests with three additional systems (AE-100, Pointer III and QRC-137 SEE-SAMS) to display the direction of a radar threat more precisely, the first six aircraft (unofficially known as EF-105Fs) left for Korat RTAFB on 28 May 1966 – less than a year after the first Phantom II shoot-down by a SAM.

Despite the Thunderchief's superior performance, the mission remained hazardous. Of the first 11 F-105Fs sent to Thailand, five had been lost by 17 August. Although their mission was still highly classified, the *Weasels'* reputation soon spread. As former Phantom II pilot Col Mike McCarthy observed, in an air force noted (like most others) for its internal rivalries, 'nobody badmouthed the *Weasels'*.

The addition of Shrike missiles (from March 1966) enabled the *Weasels* to make stand-off attacks on 'Fan Songs' rather than bombing them. Electronics companies also continued to develop improved 'black boxes'. The next batch of 18 F-105Fs had their IR-133 receivers replaced by ER-142s, which were in turn supplanted by the ER-168 (AN/APR-35) and AN/ALT-34 jamming systems. SEE-SAMS eventually appeared as the AN/ALR-31, using wingtip antennas. The QRC-160 jamming pods fitted to F-105Ds interfered with the *Weasels'* other ECM equipment, so the pod was split into two sections and scabbed onto the aircraft's belly as the QRC-288 (later QRC-335 and then AN/ALQ-105) jammer set.

This modification was central to the aircraft's re-designation as the F-105G, although many other modifications were frequently made to F-105F/Gs. These included AGM-78 Mod 0 Standard ARM capability for the F-105G, giving it a much more potent antiradiation weapon. Gen John Ryan, USAF Chief of Staff, saw the F-105G designation mainly as an administrative convenience 'to ensure that *Wild Weasel* assets can be identified in appropriate programming documents and resources allocated accordingly'.

As previously noted, the first *Weasel* crews were volunteers, including Capt (later, Lt Gen) Charles A 'Chuck' Horner, recruited by Capt Lamb. His experience in Vietnam would prove to be vital in August 1990 when, as Ninth Air Force commander, he was called in by Gen Norman

Schwartzkopf to devise an air plan to defend Saudi Arabia from invasion by Iraq. F-4G *Wild Weasels* were included from the outset in a plan which was fleshed out in an initial briefing by Col John A Warden.

STANDARD ARM

Like the Shrike, AGM-78 was a 'quick fix' US Navy programme which added the AGM-45A-3A Shrike's passive anti-radiation seeker head to the General Dynamics RIM-66A Standard surface-to-air missile. The 1370-lb missile had a range of 35 miles, allowing much safer stand-off capability than the Shrike's, and a more potent 215-lb warhead. The AGM-78A-2 (Mod 1) added a red phosphorous target marker to guide follow-up bombing attacks. A better Maxson radiation seeker, programmable for a wider bandwidth, and additional emitters had been added by the time the weapon entered service in 1968. Crucially, it had a memory circuit that enabled the missile to continue its attack on a radar which it had already locked onto, even after the radar closed down.

Although its $200,000 cost inhibited supplies, the weapon's destructive power and perhaps more importantly its deterrent value made the Standard ARM far superior to the Shrike. It entered service with a few modified US Navy A-6B Intruders in March 1968, and the USAF's 357th TFS at Takhli RTAFB received the first eight of 16 modified F-105Fs that same month after extensive trials at Eglin AFB in 1967. AGM-78A Mod 1s followed within a year, and in January 1969 the USAF redesignated all modified F-105Fs as F-105Gs, with AN/ALQ-105 jamming suites added later to many of the final 61 examples that were converted. However, the jammer could not be used against an actual SAM attack on the aircraft as it interfered with the F-105G's internal RHAW equipment.

Although the rules of engagement forbade *Weasels* from firing at SAM sites unless the latter attacked first, Lt Gen John Lavelle, Seventh Air Force commander from July 1971, stretched those rules by allowing bombing of North Vietnamese airfields and air defences. *Weasel* crews could fire at any radar site that was tracking them or aircraft they were escorting, but Lavelle argued against waiting for the *Weasel*'s radar warning receiver (RWR) gear to issue its warning. In his interpretation, hostile air defence systems were activated as soon as American aircraft entered North Vietnamese airspace, and were therefore eligible for attack.

While the US Navy sought to provoke a 'reaction' by flying heavily escorted reconnaissance aircraft over air defence sites, Lavelle relied on tacit support from his superiors to attack airfields and radar sites with Standard ARMs. However, his concern for the protection of his aircrew eventually led to his illegitimate actions being revealed to anti-war senator Harold Hughes, precipitating Lavelle's 'early retirement'. These ambivalent attitudes would not recur during the all-out assault on Iraqi defences in 1991.

A major concern, evident after the first B-52 loss to an SA-2 on 22 November 1972, was the defenders' skill in using data from their search and 'Fire Can' radars to inform the 'Fan Song' crews. This meant that *Wild Weasel* and B-52 crews were unable to detect emissions from a missile site until the last moments before a launch. A 'Fan Song' took only

F-4D-27-MC 65-0644 tested pylon installation of the AGM-78 Standard ARM at NAS Point Mugu, California, in 1967, although the weapon system would not be installed for service use. It is seen here with *Iron Hand* A-6B BuNo 151653, the Intruder introducing the AGM-78 into frontline use in early 1968 (*T Panopalis Collection*)

four seconds to activate from standby mode to full power, so battalion commanders could delay missile launching for as long as possible to defeat the *Weasels'* equipment.

Another effective avoidance technique devised by the Hanoi Air Defence Headquarters was to order several sites to briefly turn on their 'Fan Songs' when *Weasels* were approaching. Their radars could 'see' Shrikes being launched, and the 'Fan Songs' would then be turned off so that the Shrikes lost guidance. The missile was never modified with memory circuits or GPS capability to accurately attack a passive target. The AGM-45-9A did have a 'g-bias' modification to keep the missile on the same level of 'g' in its trajectory that it had been following at the point where a hostile emitter switched off, giving an improved chance of a hit.

DODGING SAMs

Wild Weasel III F-105s flew in Southeast Asia up to the last days of the Vietnam conflict in 1973. Their normal load was two Shrikes and a single AGM-78. The EWO 'Bear' strapped into the jet's rear cockpit watched for, among many other signals, a yellow 'launch' light showing that an SA-2 was airborne. He then advised the pilot on jamming, evasive action and anti-radiation missile employment.

A dive-and-turn manoeuvre to avoid a missile was basic, but when missiles appeared out of the frequent low cloud banks covering target areas there was little time for avoidance. Also, if several SA-2s were fired at once, the target aircraft had to make repeated manoeuvres that soon ran it out of energy and altitude. Each encounter required 8000 ft of clear airspace to evade a missile, which could turn at up to 4g. At low altitudes, pilots could use terrain masking to hide them from enemy radar beams, but that exposed them to AAA.

F-105Gs re-deployed to Thailand in 1972 for Operation *Linebacker I/II*, when the USAF recorded 'the most intensive use of electronic countermeasures in the Vietnam War'. Much of the *Weasels'* time was devoted to protecting the massive B-52 raids on North Vietnam. Only three confirmed kills by ARMs were recorded during the 11-day onslaught, although there were 160 cases where radars closed down in response to an ARM threat.

During Operation *Proud Deep Alpha* in December 1971, North Vietnamese radar operators discovered that they could distract an AGM-78 by shutting down the intended target radar and briefly turning on another nearby. As a result of this tactic, the expenditure of 51 Shrikes and ten AGM-78s resulted in only one GCI radar being destroyed, while 11 other 'Fan Songs' and 'Fire Cans' were 'possibly destroyed'. Clearly, a better missile was needed, and in 1969 the US Navy's Naval Weapons Center (NWC) at China Lake was already working on an ARM that would become the vastly superior AGM-88A HARM, although its development would continue until 1983, when the missile finally entered fleet service with A-7E Corsair II squadron VA-146.

PHANTOM II REPRISE

Having rejected the F-4C Phantom II in favour of the F-105F in January 1966, the USAF became increasingly aware that its diminishing fleet of F-105F/Gs was ageing fast through intensive use. Development of a *Wild Weasel* Phantom II had proceeded at a reduced rate since December 1965, when RHAW equipment was installed experimentally in an F-4C at Eglin AFB.

In 1966, 12 well-worn F-4Cs were internally equipped with Itek/ATI AN/APR-25 RHAW and AN/APR-26 launch warning receivers as *Wild Weasel IVs*. The RHAW display covered three frequency bands for SAM and AAA radars as three strobes. A solid strobe on the screen represented a low frequency source, a dashed strobe showed a middle band and a dotted strobe the upper frequency band. However, these indications did not relate to the type of radar detected, or whether it was in search or track mode.

Lack of internal space in the Phantom II's densely packed structure was the main obstacle to the whole programme, and this meant that the IR-133 panoramic receiver had to be mounted in a capsule under the rear right AIM-7 missile well. Although the RHAW and Shrike test missiles worked well at medium altitude at speeds below 460 mph, vibration caused by turbulence around the IR-133 capsule disturbed the delicate electronics at realistic combat speeds. Engineers had to find internal space for the IR-133 somehow.

Capt Everett 'Raz' Raspberry, as Project Manager for *Wild Weasel IV*, was expected to have four aircraft ready to deploy to Vietnam by the summer of 1966. However, the electronic problems that had plagued the F-4C *Wild Weasel* persisted, delaying its service entry to such an extent that two classes of crews who were training on the jet at Nellis AFB, in Nevada, for a year, but flying mainly standard F-4Cs, were sent to the 8th TFW and other Vietnam units in November 1966 to await the arrival of improved F-4Cwws. All were volunteers with at least 500 hours of flight time. Most were experienced flight leaders, while the back-seat 'Bears' primarily came from SAC units.

While they awaited their *Weasel* Phantom IIs, the first cadre flew regular F-4 missions over North Vietnam and several became MiG killers with the

The 'bug eye' antennas of the AN/APR-25 system installed in the former IR sensor fairing of F-4Cww 63-7474. The homing and omni stub antennas of the ER-142 system were installed just behind the radome, and a small blade antenna for the AN/APR-26 protruded behind the IR fairing. Other sensors were located in the tail fin cap, below the forward fuselage and on the air intake flanks (*T Panopalis Collection*)

8th TFW at Ubon RTAFB in 1967, including Capts Everett Raspberry, Dick Pascoe and Walt Radeker, and Lts Norm Wells, Dan Rafferty, Jim Murray and Frank Gullick. One EWO, Capt Ed Adcock, waited for 14 months at Ubon for the *Weasel* Phantom IIs to arrive, during which time he completed his 100-mission tour as an EB-66 crew member at Takhli RTAFB instead.

By 1968 the need for an additional *Wild Weasel* had become more urgent, and many of the F-4Cww's technical problems caused by faulty wiring and electrical interference had been resolved by using better electrical connectors and low capacitance co-axial cabling for the cockpit displays that had previously been installed in the *Weasel* F-100F and F-105F. However, it was impossible to fit the AGM-78 system into the aircraft, limiting its anti-SAM armament to two Shrikes and bombs or CBUs (the latter being far more effective at covering the widely spaced equipment at a SAM site than standard high explosive bombs). The IR-133 was replaced by an ER-142 receiver that collected information over a wider range and identified the location of radar threats quickly and accurately.

Operational testing continued into 1969 with the 4537th Fighter Weapons School. Initial test launches of ten AGM-45-9/10 Shrikes were made by Capts Stu Stegenga and Dennis B Haney at China Lake's 'Golf' Range. Shrike gave the pilot audio signals, although these were seldom useful in the dense audio traffic generated by other sources during combat.

Thirty-seven F-4Cs were eventually converted to *Wild Weasel IV-C* configuration including 63-7623, which had been a MiG killer in May 1967 for Maj John Pardo and 1Lt Steve Wayne. They were unofficially called EF-4Cs by an Air Staff Project Officer. Crew training resumed, with emphasis on the 'Bears' for the rear cockpits. Previously, the USAF had designated both F-4 crewmen as 'pilots', but *Weasel* back-seaters became EWOs. Three T-39A trainers were converted as T-39Fs for training F-4Cww and F-105G EWOs in electronic warfare at Mather AFB, California. Training against simulated 'Fan Song' and 'Fire Can' radars took place at Nellis AFB's Caliente and St George ranges, or at the US Navy's NAAS Fallon, Nevada, facility, although only three F-4Cwws were available for the *Wild Weasel* School at Nellis in 1968. Standard F-4Cs were used for much of the programme, and it involved a fair amount of air-to-air training, which was arguably irrelevant to the *Weasel* mission.

The graduates were then posted to the 81st TFS/52nd TFW at Spangdahlem AB, in West Germany, and the 347th TFW at Yokota AB, in Japan, although the latter unit was unprepared for the novelty of a *Wild Weasel* component. Its first two *Weasel* Phantom IIs arrived in April 1969, but the initial seven were treated as standard F-4Cs and distributed among its three squadrons randomly, while the trained 'weaselers' often

flew unmodified F-4Cs. Eventually all Yokota F-4Cww crews, most of whom were Vietnam-experienced, were concentrated in the 80th TFS, which became PACAF's *Wild Weasel* unit and slowly began dedicated SEAD operations. Its EWOs came from EB-66 or F-105F squadrons, while pilots had more than 1000 hrs in F-4s.

With the deactivation of the 347th TFW in May 1971, the *Weasels* moved to the 67th TFS/18th TFW at Kadena AB, on Okinawa, where the squadron was led by the highly regarded Lt Col Don Parkhurst. This assignment included two temporary deployments to Kunsan AB, in South Korea, from June 1972, which provided crews with the opportunity to test their electronic warfare (EW) skills against SAM radar systems just over the border in North Korea, as well as against friendly AAA radar sites at the Koon-ni bombing range. Pilots learned to locate hostile radars either by taking directions from the EWO's display scope or through radar indications from their two Shrike missiles. By making the two Instrument Landing System 'needles' that showed the Shrikes' detection information point straight ahead, the pilot could then use his gunsight to locate the radar. In 1971, however, they could only engage SAM sites that fired at them while flying in North Vietnam.

The deteriorating situation in Southeast Asia and North Vietnam's invasion of South Vietnam in March 1972 brought another move. The 561st TFS took its F-105Gs from McConnell AFB, Kansas, to Korat in April. Five months later, the 67th TFS was called back to Kadena from Kunsan, and six of its *Weasels* (63-7423, -7433, -7470, -7474, 64-7791 and -7840) were then sent with some of the unit's most experienced crews and Maintenance Officer Capt Larry Miller to Korat. The aircraft arrived in Thailand on 23 September to share facilities and EW duties with the F-105Gs of the 561st TFS and 17th *Wild Weasel* Squadron (formerly the 6010th WWS).

The F-4Cwws would fly their first mission on 25 September, and they were to remain in-theatre for six months while the bombing of North

F-4C-24-MC(ww) 64-0840 of the 67th TFS/ 18th TFW was photographed on arrival at Korat in September 1972 with a travel pod still on its port inner wing pylon. The jet's ER-142 azimuth and elevation antennas are positioned behind its radome, but there is no DF antenna above the wing root. Because the testing period was so complex and challenging, the final installation of highly specialised *Weasel* electronics into the Phantom II did not commence until two years after the scheduled deployment of F-4Cwws to Southeast Asia (*USAF*)

Wild Weasel IV F-4C-23-MC(ww) 64-0791 was assigned to the 67th TFS Detachment boss Lt Col Don Parkhurst and Maj Richard Taylor and also to Capts Dickie Myers and Don Triplet. Nine pilot/WSO crews at Korat flew the six available jets (two of the eight deployed were usually receiving maintenance), often flying their assigned aircraft when available. 64-0791 was christened *SQUIRRELY BIRD* due to some apparently incurable minor instability and handling problems that afflicted it. After service with the 67th TFS, this Phantom II transferred to the Indiana ANG's 113rd TFS in 1979 (*USAF*)

Vietnam resumed in earnest. A seventh F-4Cww, 64-0675, was sent to replace -7423 after a hole appeared in its cockpit floor due to corrosion. As most missions were flown at night, this was not noticed until Capts Bob Lee Tidwell and Denny Haney took it on a day sortie and the latter saw daylight, accompanied by a howling noise, through his rear cockpit floor when the landing gear was lowered. F-4Cww 63-7565 was also subsequently allocated to the Korat deployment, assigned to Capts Dick 'Dickie Duck' Myers and Don Triplet, who also flew -0675. In all, nine crews were deployed, and they usually flew their assigned jet if they were on the same flight schedule as their 'own' aircraft.

Capts Tidwell and Haney fired a total of 40 Shrikes in combat following a test firing of four near the demilitarised zone, claiming four to six electronically verifiable kills against 'Fan Songs' and ten with a high probability of a kill.

There were changes in defensive tactics by both sides. Tactical aircraft carried canisters to create chaff corridors that insulated bomber formations from hostile radar. F-4Cww crews were initially used for stand-off launching of Shrikes, although *Wild Weasels* soon began to fly 'hunter-killer' missions with F-4E Phantom II fighter-bombers – two of the latter would be paired with a single F-4Cww as flight leader. Operation *Freedom Train* in April focused on hunter-killer attacks on the SA-2 sites that had expanded into Laos, South Vietnam and southern North Vietnam.

Throughout the *Wild Weasels'* operations, like other aircrew in the Vietnam theatre, they were constantly hampered by Washington's restrictive Rules of Engagement. Thick volumes of constantly changing regulations covering approval to strike targets, no-go areas and types of ordnance that could be expended governed their lives and caused many losses and failed missions. No such bureaucratic micro-management would impede *Wild Weasel* activity in *Desert Storm* in 1991, where crews were 'cleared hot' to take out any immediate threat.

At the same time, SA-2 crews began to use 'track on jam' techniques, where a radar could be directed at the 'cloud' of electronic jamming surrounding an individual aircraft or a small formation. SA-2s could be guided towards it in the hope of causing blast damage. Radar operators were given a jam-proof tracking option with the 'Fan Song F', which had a 'bird house' cabin on its roof for an observer to track a target optically in good daylight conditions.

A new I-band ('India-band') radar signal from the Chinese version of 'Fire Can', initially dubbed T-8029, 'Team Work' or B-4272, was an unwelcome surprise in mid-1972, as it operated outside the normal range of frequencies handled by RHAW equipment. While the AGM-78C and revised AGM-45A-6 Shrike missiles could be programmed to deal with I-band transmissions, the ER-142 receiver in F-4Cwws could not detect it, putting the Phantom IIs at greater risk. Early in 1973, the ER-142 was replaced by the AN/ALR-53 Countermeasures Receiver that gave more accurate information on a wider spectrum of frequencies. At the same time, the original AN/APR-25/-26 installation gave way to the digital AN/ALR-46, comprising the superior AN/APR-36/-37 RHAW equipment, identifiable by two small antennas on the braking parachute compartment door.

Missions initially involved escorting B-52 cells over southern North Vietnam from late September 1972, and these continued as daylight sorties until the end of the war. Early flights were made in company with an F-105G leader at low altitude, which tended to run the twin-engined F-4Cww out of fuel, or a pair of F-105Gs with the F-4Cww at higher altitude. After that the Phantom II *Weasels* operated separately, usually as single aircraft, but they still escorted B-52s on most missions by day and night. Rather like Phantom II combat air patrols for B-52s, the F-4Cwws tended to orbit around areas where defences were known to be intense, rather than flanking the B-52 cells to and from their targets. SAM operators usually kept their SA-2s for the B-52s during the *Linebacker II* onslaught, so *Weasel* Phantom IIs usually found that AAA was their main enemy. On other occasions the SA-2 batteries made every effort to target the worrisome *Weasels*.

F-4C-16-MC(ww) 63-7423, previously nicknamed *Jail Bait*, is seen here on a crowded ramp at Kadena AB following the 67th TFS's return from Korat in February 1973 after a small-scale but effective combat deployment. The unit deployed to Korat again in April 1975 to cover the US withdrawal from Saigon (*T Panopalis Collection*)

WEASEL LINEBACKERS

As *Linebacker II* approached in December, the B-52 raids crept steadily northwards and targets near Vinh, a notoriously well-defended city, were hit in November. The last F-105G to be lost in the war was destroyed by a SAM near Than Hoa on 16 November. One of the B-52 crewmen involved in that mission was Maj Pete Giroux, who saw an SA-2 narrowly miss the lead bomber before a second missile 'popped through the clouds and almost immediately struck the underside of the "Thud". The ejection seats went out seconds later'. Moments earlier, Capt John Williams (EWO) and his pilot Capt Richard H Graham (who were assigned F-4Cww 63-7433 *Dick's Peace Machine*) were illuminated by a 'Fan Song' as they flew over Than Hoa, and they then saw a missile approaching. Williams later explained;

'At that point it was every man for himself, and we pushed the jet over, picked up speed and, as we pulled up, I saw the missile hit Ken and Norb's [Capt Ken Thaete and Maj Norbert Maier] F-105G in the belly and explode. Rich and I then spent the next five hours flying over the area to see if they would come up on radio.'

The three F-4Cwws in Thaete's 'Bobbin' flight were prevented by weather from providing on-site support for the downed crew, but two were able to monitor enemy radar threats from an offshore orbit for more than eight hours in total. The F-105G crew were eventually rescued by a helicopter.

The 67th TFS was initially sidelined from the first night of *Linebacker II* (18 December) by Gen John Vogt, commander Seventh Air Force, because its F-4Cwws could only carry one AN/ALQ-87 ECM pod, rather than the regulation pair for which F-105Fs and later F-4D/Es were wired. He did not want to risk the F-4Cwws in this high threat environment, but a shortage of *Weasel* aircraft for *Linebacker II* soon forced this decision to be reversed. Only 17 SEAD aircraft were available in all to support 129 B-52s.

'Hammer' flight of four F-4Cwws took off as a four-ship on the night of 19 December but flew individual orbits from positions established prior to the B-52s' arrival. Cruising at around 18,000–20,000 ft to the west of Hanoi, they detected and jammed any radars that were bold enough to 'come up'. Their Dive Modified Shrikes were unusually successful, disabling four sites and causing five others to shut down for long periods during the B-52 formation's passage overhead.

Majs Robert Belles and Palmas Kelly in 'Hammer 01' saw SAMs in flight throughout their orbits, and made repeated attempts to launch a Shrike at one site, only to have it shut down each time. Finally, they fired a missile and then turned away. As the Shrike continued its flight, the evasive 'Fan Song' was turned on again, but its emissions ceased at the estimated time of the Shrike's explosion and they did not resume. Their second Shrike also appeared to find an active 'Fan Song' and eliminate it.

Like other *Weasel* crews, Belles and Kelly had considerable difficulty in assessing the success of their attack in darkness in a threat-laden environment. One of the hazards was the possibility of being caught in the rain of bombs from the B-52s due to a communications fault. Mid-air collisions were also possible as exterior lights were switched off.

'Hammer 01' had a total of six SA-2s launched at it from two sites, but all the missiles lost guidance signals when the *Weasel's* two Shrikes

were fired at them. 'Fire Can' operators became particularly adept at identifying *Weasel* F-4Cs in their area, and they shut down at the first sign of a Shrike-launching approach. Capts Bobby Lee Tidwell and Denny Haney (in 'Hammer 04'), who were forced to fly at lower altitudes and power settings due to electronic cooling problems, counted 70 out of the 120 SA-2 launches during their mission that night. They also endured unusually heavy AAA when they tried to goad the four 257th Air Defence Regiment SA-2 batteries west of Hanoi into locking onto them.

When a missile finally rose from the 78th Missile Battalion site, Tidwell and Haney escaped it only through violent manoeuvres and survived because its proximity fuse failed to detonate. They fired both Shrikes at SAM sites and both shut down moments later. 'Hammer 03's' crew (Capts Tom Floyd and Burdette 'Al' Palmer) had similar success against two sites. The F-4Cww's first *Linebacker II* mission had proved the *Weasel* Phantom II concept, but also demonstrated the skill and courage of its crews.

On 26 December, when the final phase of Linebacker II commenced, two F-4Cww flights were tasked with B-52 protection around the north and south sides of Hanoi. The *Weasel* crews orbited over the SAM sites to the west and north of the city, including batteries near the MiG airfields at Phuc Yen and Yen Bai. They therefore faced attack by both SAMs and MiGs, although they chose to stay close to the SAM threat area which the enemy fighters would usually avoid. The two flights split up into single aircraft, monitoring SAM sites from a range of around ten miles where heavy AAA was a considerable threat. They made repeated attacks on ten sites, compelling the operators to turn on their radars long enough to provide targets for Shrikes. One of the flights (callsign 'Romeo') fired all eight of its Shrikes, claiming four radar targets hit and four others that were suppressed for the duration of the B-52 attack.

The urgency of protecting the bombers and reconnaissance aircraft meant that *Weasel* missions, previously flown almost exclusively in

Armed with a pair of Shrikes and two AIM-7E Sparrows, F-4C-18-MC(ww) 63-7474 flies over North Vietnam in December 1972, ahead of the *Linebacker II* offensive in which the unit completed more than 460 SEAD missions. The standard *Linebacker II* ordnance load was two 370-gallon underwing tanks, two Shrikes (AGM-45-3/3A/3B) on LAU-34 launchers on inboard pylons, an ECM pod in the starboard forward Sparrow bay, two AIM-7E/E2 missiles in the aft bays and chaff in the speed brakes. A centreline tank was also carried and then jettisoned when empty. This Phantom II ended its career as a battle damage repair airframe at Incirlik before being scrapped in 1995 (*USAF*)

Capts Bob Lee Tidwell and Denny Haney of the 67th TFS with F-4C-16-MC(ww) 63-7433 *DICK'S PEACE MACHINE* (assigned to Capts Dick Graham and John Williams). Heavily involved in *Linebacker II* operations, they had given the F-4Cww and Shrike combination a very effective combat introduction in September 1972 (*USAF*)

daylight, now had to be organised for poor or marginal weather at night. In those conditions, 'Lariet' flight (an F-4Cww with an F-4E) was one of five hunter-killer teams supporting B-52s on 22 December. They had to orbit above a solid 8000 ft overcast, enduring constant radar-directed AAA and avoiding attempted interception by MiG-19s and MiG-21s.

Below them were 13 SAM sites all within range, and they had to taunt the operators, persuading them to fire at the F-4s as a B-52 cell approached. As soon as a 'Fan Song' launch signal was detected they fired a Shrike, which coincided with two SA-2s heading for the lead 'Lariat' F-4Cww. Two more missiles streaked towards the B-52 cell, but all four lost guidance as the Shrike found its mark on SAM site VN-086. A follow-up CBU attack by the 'Lariet' F-4E was made through thick cloud and heavy AAA.

When a second site fired three missiles at the B-52s, 'Lariet 01' (Capts Floyd and Palmer, whose assigned jet was nicknamed *Brain Damage*) fired a second Shrike in a dive. It was the target of considerable AAA when the *Weasel* pulled up. Their partner F-4E followed, penetrating the same storm of AAA to drop more CBUs on the site, taking it out of contention. The pair continued to circle in this intensely hostile area, faking more attacks on other sites to distract them from the incoming B-52 waves. It was estimated that they evaded or neutralised up to 50 SA-2s that night.

Generally, the F-4Cwws on night hunter-killer missions orbited almost overhead SAM sites at 15,000 to 17,000 ft, while CBU-52-armed F-4Es were stacked above them at 21,000–23,000 ft, looking for the smoke target-marker from a Shrike explosion before diving to attack.

During the first four nights of the campaign, it seemed that half of the 11 B-52s lost to SAMs were victims of a single 'Team Work' SA-2 site using radar frequencies that had previously only appeared from 'Fire Can' AAA radars. The site was identified as VN-549, manned by an expert crew, and it was singled out for heavy attack by *Weasels* and B-52s. On the fifth night, F-111As of the 474th TFW bombed SAM sites to support the ten

F-4C-16-MC(ww) 63-7423 *Jail Bait* of the 67th TFS tops off its tanks prior to delivering Shrikes against hostile radars. The jet's light tan ER-142 antennas are scabbed onto the nose (just aft of the black radome), from where they collected accurate long-range azimuth information. This Phantom II was assigned to Capt William C McLeod II and Maj Donald J Lavigne, who chose a nickname that reflected the dangers into which the jet could take its crew (*John Huggins Collection*)

pairs of F-105G and F-4Cww hunter-killer teams. Some of the 'Fire Cans' that appeared to be linked to the SA-2 sites were situated in the 'no go' Chinese buffer zone on the border of North Vietnam. One was probably hit by an F-4Cww crewed by Capt William McLeod and Maj Don Lavigne on Night 6, using AGM-45A-6 Shrikes tuned to the I-band wavelength.

The efforts of the small *Weasel* contingent were not always appreciated. Gen John C Meyer, commander-in-chief of SAC, stated that the B-52 losses were caused largely by inadequate SAM suppression rather than the inappropriate tactics of his own mission planners. He felt that direct attacks on SA-2 sites by B-52s, F-111s and US Navy A-6 Intruders would have been more effective. Gen Vogt contended that the *Weasels'* main problem was having to fight at night, meaning that they had to expend most of their ordnance in pre-emptive shots at suspected SAM sites prior to the B-52s' arrival. Gen Lucius D Clay, commander-in-chief of the Pacific Air Forces, suggested that some of the B-52 raids should be made in daylight so that the *Weasel* F-4Cwws and F-105Gs could see and attack the sites more easily. However, persistent bad weather at the time reduced visibility considerably in any case.

The crews were faced with SA-2s launched in various ways – a few with fully automatic 'Fan Song' guidance, some with information from other radar systems in a network and others without any guidance at all. Although the Vietnamese Peoples' Air Force lacked night capability, MiG-21s were occasionally sent to attempt interceptions of B-52s. One was vectored onto an F-4Cww on the night of 20 December, but the Phantom II pilot, Capt Tom Floyd, saw its head-on approach and turned behind the jet, launching an AIM-7 Sparrow missile at the MiG. Typically, the weapon failed to guide correctly.

Flying at night raised its own problems, including glare from cockpit instrument displays and warning lights that could disturb the crew's

F-4C(ww)s 64-0840 *SUPER COCKS SWISS SAMLAR* and 64-0675 take on fuel from a KC-135A in 1973. The 67th TFS's *DDD&CC* logo is repeated on the vari-ramps of both jets. The unit saw much of its combat during *Linebacker II* at night (*T Panopalis Collection*)

vision outside the cockpit. Pilots would often set up their controls and switches and then tape over anything that produced distracting light. Moonlight was sometimes bright enough to read maps as a back-up to visual navigation. Aircrew in *Desert Storm* two decades later, with even more sophisticated navigation aids, had to use the same trick, and they also taped over distracting lights. Seeing a SAM site was a difficult but vital part of a daylight SEAD mission, as was the need to spot if a missile had hit its target. At night a crew was unlikely to be able to see more than the dazzling flash of its own missile launches.

Linebacker II was an opportunity to refine the hunter-killer teams of F-4Cwws and F-4Es. The latter had previously flown as teams with F-105Gs, but the F-4C's performance made it a more suitable partner. For B-52 raids involving a single wave flying against targets that were close to each other, it was possible to provide five hunter-killer pairs.

During their tour, the comparatively elderly F-4Cs created plenty of work for their maintenance crews who were used to more recent F-4D/E Phantom IIs, but there were no losses. However, the jet's avionics suite was dated by late 1972, leaving the aircraft unable to cope with the rapidly expanding range of threat radars and frequencies that Soviet manufacturers were devising. Its lack of ability to handle the Standard ARMs was always a disadvantage, remedied in 1978 by the introduction of the F-4G *Wild Weasel*. Mounting the Standard ARM on an F-4Cww was also impossible because it prevented the aircraft's flaps from lowering fully. F-4Gs did not require full flaps.

Compared with the F-105G, the F-4Cww was considered 'noisy, poorly air conditioned and not terribly stable in the air' according to former Thunderchief *Weasel* pilot Maj Jerry Stiles. One major source of distracting noise for the rear-seater was the external rear-view mirror above the canopy bow, which generated a roaring sound at high speed and was eventually removed. Phantom IIs did have the advantage of two engines and a cockpit configuration that was intended to work around the 'team concept' for the crew, rather than the F-105G, where the pilot usually adhered to the single-seat philosophy due to the jet effectively being a converted trainer. The F-4Cww also offered slightly better visibility for the WSO from the rear seat compared with the F-105G.

Despite the acute and increasing threat from SA-2s, only around 150 F-4Cwws, F-105Gs and F-100Fs were modified for the anti-SAM role, and even at the most intense stages of the war the total number of *Wild Weasel* aircrew in-theatre never exceeded 75. The dangers of the role were emphasised by the loss of 68 aircrew, including 30 who were killed in action and 19 who became prisoners of war. Only 17 were rescued.

The last 67th TFS mission was flown on 16 February 1973, and the squadron returned to Kadena two days later after completing 460 combat sorties without loss. Ten of the squadron's 16 F-4Cwws briefly deployed to Korat from 20 April 1975 to provide cover for Operation *Frequent Wind* – the US withdrawal from Saigon. The unit was forced to deploy to Thailand because US aircraft were not allowed to fly in combat from Japanese bases. Some of the Phantom IIs involved in the operation were reassigned from a regular *Commando Domino* air defence detachment at Ching Chuan Kang AB, in Taiwan.

The F-4Cwws normally carried two AGM-45s, two AIM-7 Sparrows, an AN/ALQ-87 ECM pod and two 370-gallon wing tanks. Teamed with 34th TFS/388th TFW F-4D Phantom IIs armed with four CBU-52 canisters on their centreline racks, they patrolled areas around Saigon and Bien Hoa within 20 miles of Tan Son Nhut AB's radar coverage from mid-morning to mid-afternoon, suppressing AAA and attacking NVA forces only if they were fired on.

By 22 April the build-up of enemy forces warranted a change in the Rules of Engagement to allow attacks on any 'Fan Songs' that posed a threat. While on station, three offshore in-flight refuelling sessions were needed to maintain the coverage – some top ups from the duty tanker had to be aborted due to bad weather or poor coordination. There was a great deal of confusion about North Vietnamese intentions and their likely interference in the evacuation. The presence of numerous South Vietnamese aircraft in the skies over Saigon, some possibly flown by North Vietnamese pilots with hostile intent, added to the challenging nature of the *Frequent Wind* missions.

A successful attack on a gun battery was made by one of the F-4Ds, which had been guided to the target by a Shrike from the 'Miller' flight F-4Cww of Capts Jack 'Jay' Suggs and John Dewey. The latter had been fired on during their third and final orbit near a 'Fan Song' which had lured them into a 'flak trap' comprising around ten 57 mm guns. Suggs fired an unguided Shrike as a target-marking rocket for Maj Bob Bolls' F-4D. The CBUs took out several of the guns and their ammunition pit, these

Roll-out of Advanced *Wild Weasel V* prototype 66-7647 took place at McDonnell Douglas' St Louis, Missouri, plant on 19 January 1972. It was one of two F-4D-29-MCs flown as testbed aircraft for the AN/APR-38A homing and warning computer at Edwards AFB, California, with components housed in an enlarged IR sensor under the nose and in any other available space within the already crammed fuselage (*T Panopalis Collection*)

bombs being the last ordnance delivered by US tactical aircraft in Vietnam. Removing the guns brought an AAA ceasefire that allowed many more helicopters to evacuate personnel safely from Saigon. The Phantom IIs returned to Kadena on 2 May, although four had a false start due to tanker problems. One of the war-weary aircraft lost its cockpit canopy on approach to Kadena.

Post-war, some F-4Cwws were allocated to Air National Guard (ANG) units after being stripped of their *Weasel* equipment, the jets ending their careers as bomb-damage repair airframes or display items. Only two had been lost, both in operational accidents unrelated to combat over Vietnam.

F-4Ds 65-0657 and -0660 were involved in Stage IV-B of the *Weasel* programme to test the Bendix APS-107 RHAW system as an alternative to the APR-25/-26, although it proved less reliable despite giving the F-4C/D the potential to carry the AGM-78 Standard ARM. It was eventually fitted in all F-4Ds. Gen John D Ryan wanted an avionics system, preferably for the F-4D, that would 'satisfy future *Wild Weasel* requirements while still retaining the capability to perform the basic tactical fighter role'.

Test-firing of the AGM-78 was conducted by F-4D 65-0644, and other D-model jets were used to test the AGM-65 Maverick air-to-ground missile and the AN/APR-38 warning and attack system. Both subsequently became essential elements of the *Wild Weasel V* programme. Development then suffered from delays in procuring reliable power supply units for some of the EW equipment. The central computer needed replacement by a more powerful model, delaying the programme further into 1974. Although the three test-bed EF-4Ds (66-7635, 66-7647 and 66-7648) remained in use with versions of the AN/APR-38, plans for a further 90 F-4Ds to carry the revised *Wild Weasel* fit were cancelled when the USAF decided to use later F-4Es for the role, the 'new' jets being redesignated F-4Gs.

CHAPTER THREE

ULTIMATE *WEASELS*

part from its Southeast Asian commitments, the USAF was still focused on its NATO role in Europe, and a SEAD component was introduced to its armoury with the F-4Cww when 12 examples were delivered to the 81st TFS/50th TFW at Hahn AB, in West Germany, from December 1969. Within a period of frequent USAFE unit movements, the squadron was detached to Zweibrucken AB, also in West Germany, in June 1971 for the 86th TFW, and then on to the 52nd TFW at Spangdahlem AB in January 1973, where the 81st remained until July 1979 when the veteran Phantom IIs were replaced by F-4Gs.

During that time the F-4Cwws' AN/APR-25/-26 and ER-142 equipment was replaced by a digital AN/ALR-46 radar warning receiver and AN/ALR-53 countermeasures receiver. Many other minor cockpit modifications had also occurred so that there was some variety in configuration between individual aircraft.

81st TFS EWOs trained at George AFB, in California, initially found the European scenario sadly deficient in EW training facilities. Spadeadam Electronic Tactics Warfare Range in Cumbria offered the widest variety of radar emissions, but they were all located close together, denying the crews essential practice in locating diverse threats. The Tonopah range in Nevada had a wider spread of simulated radar threats, but they were not camouflaged and soon became predictable targets in repetitive training sorties. That situation was resolved to a great extent from 1979 with the

F-4C-16-MC(ww) 63-7440 was assigned to the 81st TFS/52nd TFW at Spangdahlem, its Vietnam camouflage blending well with the West German landscape. The squadron's *Weasel* F-4Cs had been replaced by F-4Gs by the end of July 1979. This example then moved to the Indiana ANG's 163rd TFS/122nd TFW along with 16 other former F-4Cwws, where the aircraft were flown as conventional Phantom IIs. The ANG had no *Wild Weasel* responsibilities until it received F-4Gs (*T Panopalis Collection*) development of the Polygone EW training range on several sites along the Franco-German border. Operated by both countries and USAFE, the range provided realistic scenarios and gave *Weasel* crews experience of Soviet-type radar defences.

Visits to *Red Flag* exercises in the USA were considered particularly valuable, and they led to a *Green Flag* series which concentrated on EW. F-4Gs carrying training rounds of Maverick and anti-radar missiles were pitted against portable radars that could simulate a range of Soviet systems. Multiple Threat Emitter Simulators and 'Smoky Sam' pyrotechnics to simulate man-portable air defence systems (MANPADS) with small, infra-red (IR) homing missiles were added, while other EW types joined the wargame simulations.

Concerns were expressed about the Phantom II's survivability at low altitudes against Soviet AAA in view of Vietnam experience. However, the *Weasels'* services, like those of the EB-66C/E jamming aircraft that joined USAFE in West Germany in 1969, were increasingly in demand as Soviet forces introduced more sophisticated radar networks. When they were replaced by F-4Gs, the F-4Cwws were mostly passed to the Indiana ANG's 163rd TFS/122nd TFW, where they flew as standard F-4Cs until they gave way to F-4Es in the spring of 1988. The surviving F-105Gs, meanwhile, had also been passed on to the ANG, and their last sorties were flown in May 1983. Many of the Thunderchiefs had the AN/ALR-46 system fitted during their final period of service.

WILD WEASEL V

Following the cancellation of the F-4D *Wild Weasel* project, the need for an effective SEAD aircraft was very soon emphasised by the struggles of the Israeli Phantom II squadrons in the War of Attrition and Yom Kippur conflicts of the late 1960s and early 1970s. Opposed by the very effective Soviet SA-3 'Goa' and SA-6 'Gainful' SAMs and a variety of new short-range missiles, the F-4E pilots discovered that their AN/ALQ-101 ECM pods were unable to cope with this opposition. Concerted attacks on Israel's airfields on 6 October 1973 by Egyptian, Iraqi and Syrian fighter-bombers triggered an Israeli response which cost them six F-4Es, downed by a wall of missiles and AAA ranged along the west bank of the Suez Canal.

Although the Israeli Air Force (IAF) had Shrike missiles in its arsenal, the opposition learned the lessons of Vietnam and kept their radars inactive to frustrate retaliation from above. Despite three SAM batteries being destroyed and five damaged, the losses continued – some 50 IAF aircraft had been shot down within three days, mainly by 2K12 (SA-6 'Gainful') SAMs and the deadly ZSU-23-4 Shilka radar-guided, four-barrel 23 mm anti-aircraft weapons supplied by Moscow. The SA-6 was able to operate against targets flying as low as 150 ft, the SAM being controlled by a linked network of radars including 'Spoon Rest' and 'Side Net' height-finding equipment. When IAF jets attempted to avoid SA-6 batteries by descending below 100 ft, they then fell prey to AAA that was always ready to catch low-flying aircraft as they sped over fairly level territory in good daylight conditions.

At those altitudes pilots also faced SA-7 'Strela' IR-guided, shoulder-launched MANPADS that could only be deflected by carefully timed flares. Large numbers of fighters were also directed at the IAF's Phantom IIs as they tried to neutralise enemy defences. However, some solutions were found, including the well-established practice of spreading chaff from externally mounted dispensers to distract radar-guided missiles. Helicopters with jammers aboard were also flown near known radar sites and long-range artillery was directed at them.

Fully loaded, tracked, SA-6 'Gainful' SAM launchers, with an SA-3 'Goa' battery at far left, await inspection by senior officers of the Egyptian Army in the months prior to the Yom Kippur War of October 1973. More advanced than the SA-2, both SAM systems were responsible for a significant number of the 50 IAF fighter-bombers lost in the opening three days of fighting in the October conflict (*DoD*)

Probably the most innovative tactic, and the most influential in the long term, was the use of BQM-34A Firebee reconnaissance drones to fly close to SAM sites. Radar operators were often persuaded to switch on and engage them, thereby attracting Shrikes and free-fall ordnance from lurking strike aircraft. Eventually, like the North Vietnamese defenders in 1972, Egypt and Syria ran out of SAMs and the IAF was able to provide close support for an Israeli counter-invasion force which was enabled by the destruction of most of the remaining air defences.

This entirely convincing demonstration of the crucial importance of SEAD was a powerful influence in the adoption of a new USAF advanced *Wild Weasel* programme. By that time the F-4D variant was out of production, and Maj Jerry Stiles suggested using the F-4E as the basis of a new *Wild Weasel* platform. His recommendation was influenced by the extreme difficulty of finding internal space in the F-4C/D for the *Weasel* electronics. Even the small and inaccessible space between the two engines was required for electronics in the F-4D testbeds.

The key to the new *Weasel* variant's role was its AN/APR-38 weapons system, produced by IBM Federal Systems (with components from Dalmo Victor, Loral, Texas Instruments, IBM and McDonnell Douglas) under the *Pave Strike* programme. The F-4E at least offered the internal space occupied by its M61A1 gun and ammunition store, with room in the fairing beneath the nose for new electronic black boxes. Receiver and transmitting antennas had to be located at 52 locations on various parts of the airframe, including phased interferometer arrays in the nose area and in a pod attached to the top of the vertical stabiliser. Potential antenna placement below the gun was ruled out due to vibration. A position above the nose interfered with the pilot's vision and removal of the AN/APQ-120 radar to offer space was quickly discounted.

Sacrificing the gun was therefore inevitable. This was greeted with understandable opposition from those who had fought hard to get a gun into the Phantom II, but it had to go. Maj Stiles suggested the designation 'F-4W' to reflect the *Weasel* role more obviously, (*text continues on page 45*)

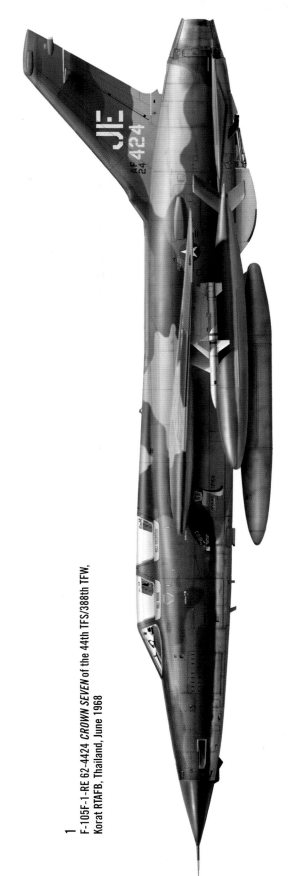

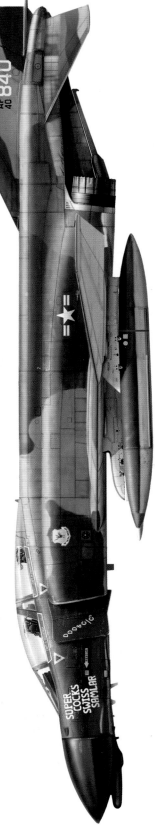

1
F-105F-1-RE 62-4424 *CROWN SEVEN* of the 44th TFS/388th TFW,
Korat RTAFB, Thailand, June 1968

2
F-4C-24-MC(ww) 64-0840 *SUPER COCKS SWISS SAMLAR* of the
67th TFS/18th TFW, Korat RTAFB, Thailand, November 1972

3
F-4C-18-MC(ww) 63-7470 *RUB-A-DUB-DUB, TWO MEN IN A TUB* of the
67th TFS/18th TFW, Korat RTAFB, Thailand, December 1972

4
F-4C-23-MC(ww) 64-0757 of the 67th TFS/18th TFW,
Kadena AFB, Okinawa, 1972

5
F-4G 69-7295-44-MC of the 81st TFS/52nd TFW, Spangdahlem AB,
West Germany, 1979

6
F-4G-44-MC 69-7287 of the 561st TFS/35th TFW,
George AFB, California, August 1987

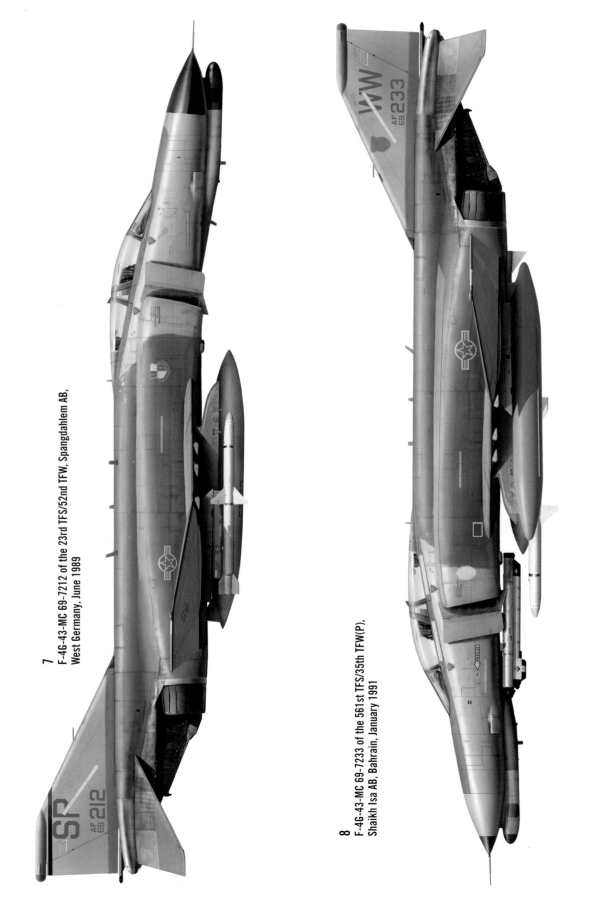

7
F-4G-43-MC 69-7212 of the 23rd TFS/52nd TFW, Spangdahlem AB,
West Germany, June 1989

8
F-4G-43-MC 69-7233 of the 561st TFS/35th TFW(P),
Shaikh Isa AB, Bahrain, January 1991

9
F-4G-42-MC 69-0244 *Night Stalker* of the 23rd TFS/7440th CW(P),
Incirlik AB, Turkey, February 1991

10
F-4G-42-MC 69-0254 of the 561st TFS/4404th CW(P),
Dhahran AB, Saudi Arabia, February 1992

11
F-4G-43-MC 69-7211 of the 81st TFS/4404th CW(P), Dhahran AB,
Saudi Arabia, February 1992

12
F-4G-42-MC 69-0298 of the 190th FS/124th FG (Idaho ANG)
assigned to the 7440th CW(P), Incirlik AB, December 1995

13
F-4G-43-MC 69-7232 of the 561st FS/57th Wing, Dhahran AB,
Saudi Arabia, January 1996

14
F-4G-42-MC 69-0260 of the 23rd FS/7440th CW(P),
Incirlik AB, Turkey, early 1991

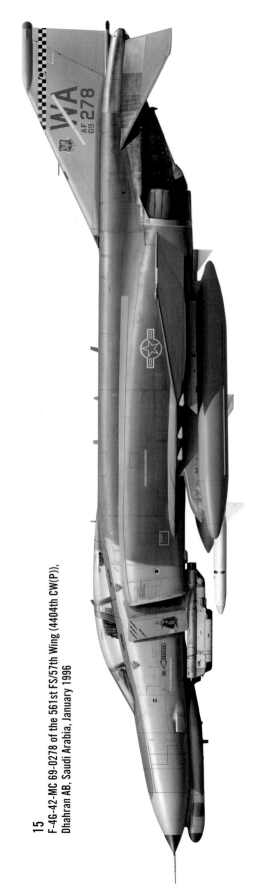

15
F-4G-42-MC 69-0278 of the 561st FS/57th Wing (4404th CW(P)),
Dhahran AB, Saudi Arabia, January 1996

16
F-4G-42-MC 69-0265 of the 561st TFS/35th TFW(P), Shaikh Isa AB,
Bahrain, January 1991

17
F-4G-45-MC 69-7579 of the 561st FS/57th Wing (4404th CW(P)),
Dhahran AB, Saudi Arabia, January 1996

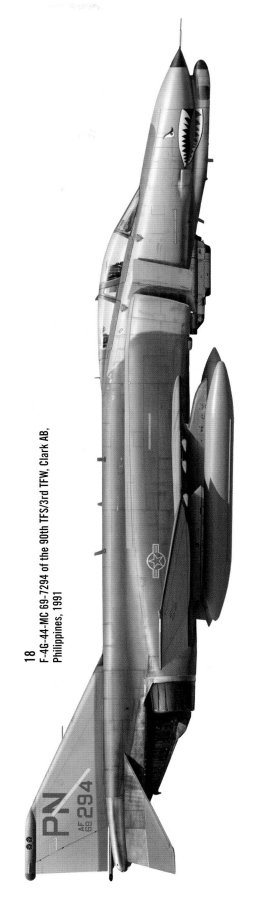

18
F-4G-44-MC 69-7294 of the 90th TFS/3rd TFW, Clark AB,
Philippines, 1991

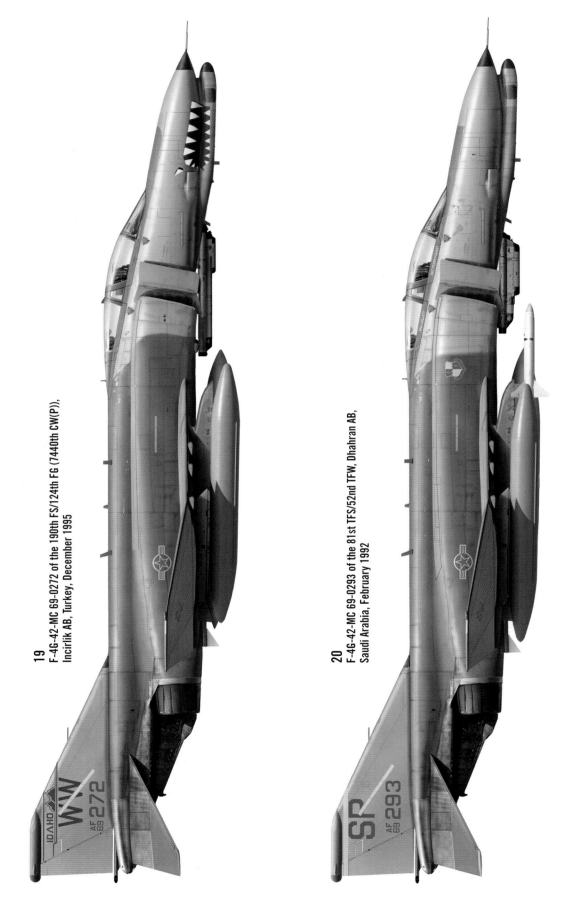

19
F-4G-42-MC 69-0272 of the 190th FS/124th FG (7440th CW(P)),
Incirlik AB, Turkey, December 1995

20
F-4G-42-MC 69-0293 of the 81st TFS/52nd TFW, Dhahran AB,
Saudi Arabia, February 1992

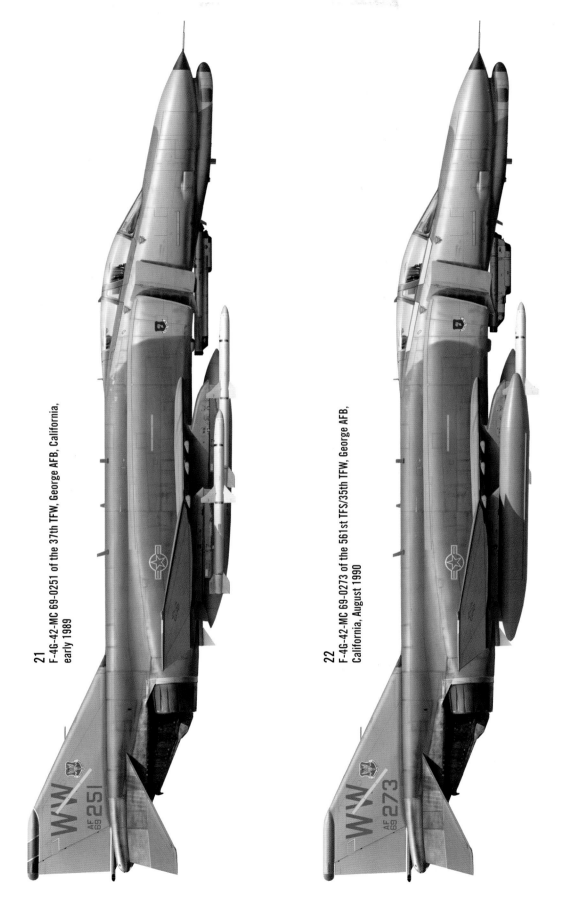

21
F-4G-42-MC 69-0251 of the 37th TFW, George AFB, California, early 1989

22
F-4G-42-MC 69-0273 of the 561st TFS/35th TFW, George AFB, California, August 1990

44

23
F-4G-44-MC 69-7556 of the 81st TFS/52nd TFW, Shaikh Isa AB,
Bahrain, March 1991

24
F-4G-43-MC 69-7235 of Detachment 5 of the 4485th TES, Tactical
Air Warfare Centre, Eglin AFB, Florida, 1987

YF-4G-43-MC 69-7254, which served as the F-4G testbed, taxies out at Edwards AFB in February 1976. After its first flight, on 6 December 1975, the jet received two major updates to its test AN/APR-38 computer system before being delivered to George AFB in 1979 for frontline use, initially with the 35th TFW. Placed in storage at AMARC in June 1992, the aircraft was converted into a QF-4G drone in 1999 and expended as a missile target in June 2002 (*T Panopalis Collection*)

but 'F-4G' was chosen, continuing the F-105G tradition despite the previous, brief, use of the F-4G label for a data-link equipped version of the US Navy F-4B Phantom II. Installation of the AN/APR-38 system had little effect on the aircraft's handling, although Col Jim Uken pointed out that it made the aircraft a little heavier in the nose than the F-4E, causing 'a tendency to bleed off airspeed a little more when going uphill and, conversely, accelerating a little faster when going downhill'.

The work and sacrifice of the previous *Wild Weasel* pioneers had established SEAD as an acknowledged necessity in the armoury, although the USAF was still unwilling to commission a purpose-built aircraft for the role, rather than a conversion of an in-service type. Its mission was very clear, however. As Maj Stiles put it, the *Weasels'* primary role was 'unmitigated, no holds barred, bare knuckled intimidation'. Making the enemy ground defences 'respect and honour' the presence of a *Weasel* meant showing him that; 'If he wanted to hurt someone, he had to realise that he was liable to get bruised in exchange.'

After an initial mock-up installation of the AN/APR-38 in YF-4E 65-0713, the YF-4G *Wild Weasel V* testbed (69-7254), converted from a slat-winged F-4E, was ready to fly on 6 December 1975, eventually followed by the first production F-4G (69-0239) on 28 April 1978.

The aircraft's AN/APR-38 installation worked well in operation, offering many advantages over previous systems. It could detect, analyse and 'label' hostile emitters, prioritising the principal 15 threats (with assistance from its computer menu of threats) and displaying them in the rear cockpit as symbols on plan position indicator (PPI) screens. The most immediate threat was highlighted by a brighter triangle symbol. The EWO could place a diamond-shaped cursor over a threat symbol, which would then show its range and bearing (calculated by triangulation), together with the Phantom II's magnetic heading. AAA sites were indicated by an 'A' symbol, SA-3 sites by '3' and unidentified threats by a 'J'. It could also remember threats so that a *Weasel* crew could perform evasive tactics and return for a re-attack against multiple targets. All digital and voice data from a mission was recorded for later analysis.

The AN/APR-38 was the first radar and attack warning system specifically designed for the *Wild Weasel* mission. It gave 360-degree coverage, which was lacking in the later F-16 *Wild Weasel* version. It derived data from a range of inputs, including the aircraft's position in the air, its weapons and their fire control systems, so that it could indicate the best attack modes allowing for the range, launch limits and other characteristics of those weapons.

Navigation was handled by the AN/ARN-101(V) Digital Modular Avionics System, retro-fitted in 1986 and known as 'Arny' in service (or sometimes as 'Garny' in its F-4G application). It had initially been installed in some F-4Es and RF-4Cs from 1978. The AN/ARN-101(V) gave much greater accuracy in bombing and navigation than the previous inertial navigation system (INS). The long-range navigation equipment used in contemporary F-4Es and RF-4Cs was considered unnecessary.

This early 35th TFW F-4G is carrying an AGM-45C Shrike, an AGM-78D Standard ARM and an AN/ALQ-119(V)-17 ECM pod. The aircraft's distinctive leading-edge wing slats originated from the USAF's Project *Agile Eagle 1* in response to the Phantom II's tendency to enter a stall-spin when subjected to sharp manoeuvres and 'pop-up' climbs. They improved handling at low altitudes, where the F-4G was originally scheduled to operate (*USAF*)

The EWO could also take over any aspect of this process manually and issue specific commands to the computer regarding weapons and search schemes. Both occupants had Loral PPI screens, controlled by the EWO, that displayed the position of a threat radar, and its distance, relative to the F-4G. EWOs also had a panoramic analysis display and a screen for a homing indicator. An EWO was also responsible for operating chaff and flare countermeasures dispensers from Tracor AN/ALE-40 30-tube boxes attached to the underwing pylons. He managed weapons controls, jamming pods, radio and TACAN controls, as well as the radar in air-to-air and air-to-ground modes. He also had a set of flying controls, but virtually no forward vision to allow him to use them effectively. In the front cockpit, the pilot had a single 12-inch repeater scope to show him what the EWO was seeing on his much larger PPI and control display.

F-4G cockpits had a carefully designed standard layout that was in marked contrast to the variety of modified layouts seen in F-4Cwws. This helped with one of the most demanding aspects of the crew's role – the tendency to suffer from task saturation when faced with an extremely complex combat environment in which both members had to perform their tasks accurately and cope with a constantly varying range of threats. As with previous *Weasel* crews, the pilot and WSO pairing in an F-4G had to have an intimate knowledge of each other's tasks and the ability to coordinate their actions, despite the many distractions they faced.

In combat, an EWO would have the added responsibility of watching for aerial threats from fighters aft of the wing, while the pilot checked the area ahead of the 'wing line'. In *Desert Storm*, where the threat from enemy fighters was essentially removed by Coalition interceptors, an EWO could safely keep his eyes on his cockpit displays. As Capt Gary Gray of the 52nd FW commented, 'The *Wild Weasel* mission was specifically the 'EWO's' job'. As pilot, Gray was tasked with getting the aircraft safely to and from the target, as the F-4G crew would probably be the 'first in and last out'. He also had to visually detect any aerial or ground threats.

Orders for 116 F-4Gs followed in 1976, although 134 conversions (each taking 110 days) from the 1970 production Block 42/45 F-4Es were eventually allowed, using aircraft with low airframe hours. Thirty had previously been loaned to the Royal Australian Air Force (RAAF), pending the delivery of F-111Cs, or leased to Iran. The second batch of 18, converted at the Ogden Air Logistics Center at Hill AFB, in Utah, and ordered partly as attrition replacements, were painted in the USAF's new two-tone Hill Gray colours that were eventually sprayed on all F-4Gs.

The second batch all had the updated AN/APR-47 in place of the AN/APR-38 as part of the first Performance Update Program (PUP-1). That system, also retrofitted to earlier F-4Gs, had three times the computer memory and a new *Weasel* Attack Signal Processor. All these former F-4Es had been manufactured before the Northrop ASX-1 TISEO (target identification system, electro-optical) was installed in the E-model's left wing, and they were the only remaining suitable Fiscal 1969 jets that were available for *Weasel* conversion.

AN/APR-47 was the key to the F-4G's success, as pilot Capt Bruce Benyshek explained in 1992;

'The -47 is a very sophisticated receiver that determines an emitter's location by analysing the angle of arrival of a signal and then triangulating any additional emissions from that site. The triangulation is performed by a powerful computer in the -47 that is tied to the INS. The -47 gives both crew members a 360-degree picture of emissions around the aircraft. Should the tactical situation call for us to employ a HARM, the EWO will designate the site and "hand off" to the missile – i.e. transfer various bits of information about the site to the missile. These parameters will be used by the missile to find the target. Having done this, the missile is ready to shoot.

'Actual employment of the weapon is an impressive sight. At "pickle" [release], there is a resounding "clunk" as the missile comes off the rail. Usually, the pilot's first view of the weapon is when it is already 1000 ft in front of the aircraft – this is a fast missile! After launch, the system is entirely passive, so we are free to do as we please. There is no lock-on we must maintain.'

'Spike' Benyshek and his EWO, Capt Larry Allen, scored five confirmed radar kills during *Desert Storm*.

WEASEL WEAPONS

The F-4G could carry most of the USAF's tactical ordnance for ground attack and self-defence. It was even wired for gun pods under the wings, although these were not used in action. Shrike continued as an option for the F-4G, and some remaining rounds were expended by aircraft in February 1991 *Desert Storm* missions, but the AGM-78 Standard was its initial primary weapon, including the AGM-78D-2 version which could be fired 'off boresight' so that the aircraft did not have to be pointing directly at the target.

The F-4G could also carry the AGM-65A/B Maverick air-to-ground missile, which was first tested for compatibility in 1969. Optically guided Mavericks were usually fired by the EWO who fed enough information into the missile (using the radar scope display at the base of his main cockpit panel and his radar 'slew' handle) to enable it to lock on to a target. After launch, it became a 'fire and forget' missile.

Electro-optically guided versions of the Mk 84 bomb were also available, but CBU-52 or CBU-58 units were more usually loaded. The CBU-87/D dispenser with 214 BLU-97 combined-effects munitions, which was used for combat in the Middle East conflicts of the early 1990s, was loaded in pairs on each inboard pylon of F-4Es or F-4Gs.

81st TFS F-4G-43-MC 69-7202 on 'finals' in August 1982 with a Maverick training round aboard. The pilot would usually deploy a braking parachute upon landing back at Spangdahlem during peacetime flying. However, in Operation *Desert Shield/ Storm* F-4Gs sometimes landed without deploying the 'chute after having to divert to a base that had no parachute packing facility. Such landings could only be attempted on runways that had a length of at least 12,000 ft, such as Shaikh Isa (*Author's Collection*)

Col Uken, who used an AGM-65 to destroy an Iraqi PRV-9 'Thin Skin' height-finding radar, pointed out that a Maverick had to be fired from much closer in and at lower altitudes than an AGM-88 HARM 'due to the requirement to place the target in the missile's narrow field of view. You located the target on your radar scope, converted to a TV picture. You tracked the threat, physically identified the target, locked on to it [in this case using the Maverick's IR picture] and then made sure the Maverick "saw" the picture it was locked on to before firing. I estimate that our shot was probably taken at about two to two-and-a-half miles out'.

HARM

The advent of the Texas Instruments AGM-88A High-Speed Anti-Radiation Missile (HARM) gave the F-4G its primary weapon after the missile's service entry in 1983 with A-7E-equipped VA-146. As another US Navy initiative, work on the weapon commenced at NWC China Lake in 1969 and it was test-flown from 1975. F-4G squadrons had stopped using the AGM-78 Standard ARM by early 1983 in anticipation of the arrival of HARM.

A far more powerful internal computer was the key to the new weapon's ability to be pre-programmed with the priorities, types and locations of a range of emitter targets, all of which could be tweaked or changed in flight. Much lighter than the Standard ARM at 800 lbs, the HARM could be launched at a distance of more than 40 miles from the target. Although the fragmentation warhead weighed only 125 lbs, it could be delivered with great accuracy and travel at much higher speeds than its predecessors, thus ensuring destruction of the target. In tests, the HARM achieved a 75 per cent success rate after adjustments to its seeker that enabled it to differentiate between emissions from a hostile source and reflections of those emissions from other surfaces. In service, the HARM was nicknamed the 'wish you were dead' weapon due to its accuracy, and ability to beat attempts to avoid it.

The AGM-88B was introduced in 1984. It could be fully programmed at an air base rather than having to be sent to a technical maintenance centre for such work to be carried out. HARM could be launched in one of three semi-automatic modes, and crucially, unlike the Shrike, it could

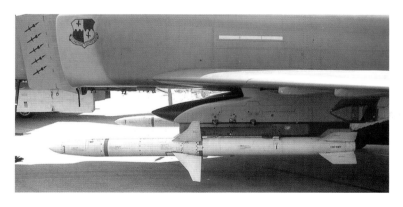

The ATM-88B was the inert training version of the 13 ft-long HARM, distinguished by a blue band between the guidance section and the warhead. The same pylon had an AN/ALE-40 chaff and flare dispenser attached to its rear edge. At $200,000 per round (2020 prices), HARM still represented good value on the basis of the 'one shot, one kill' reputation it earned in action (*Author's Collection*)

be re-programmed in flight. In Self-Protect mode, the weapon was fired after the aircraft's internal ECM and fire control systems detected and prioritised an imminent threat as a target of opportunity. The AN/APR-38 (or later AN/APR-47) computer then generated steering data and fired the HARM. It climbed to gain altitude and increase its range, homing onto the target even if the weapon was fired with the aircraft pointing away from it.

Firing a HARM at night created a blinding white light, and smoke from the weapon would often enter the engine air inlet, causing a burning smell to permeate the cockpit unless the pilot rolled the aircraft slightly away from the missile launch. The HARM was 'pickled' by pressing a switch on the control column after it had received target data from the AN/APR-47 in a process called the 'hand-off'. This was accomplished by pressing a button close to the AN/APR-47 display, waiting for a ready light to show that the information had been received by the AGM-88's memory and then firing the missile after mutual consent between front and back seaters.

Fired in Target of Opportunity mode, the missile's seeker could detect an unknown threat and display it on the pilot's warning panel so that he had the chance to command the weapon to make an attack. The third option ('range known') sent the missile against a selection of potential targets for which it had been pre-programmed before take-off. It could be fired towards the likely location of those known emitters in the hope that one of them would 'come up' while it was in the air. HARM would then home onto that target.

In daylight combat at low altitude, pilots learned to divert the aircraft away from the launch point straight away, as AAA gunners could otherwise use the missile's thick, white smoke trail as a visual guide leading back to the launch aircraft. At night, they could use the flash of a HARM launch as an aiming point. Pilots also made guidance radars break lock, or at least stay active for longer periods, by flying a course that ran perpendicular to the radiation source, rather than towards it.

F-4Gs could retain the Phantom II's normal air-to-air armament of four AIM-9 Sidewinders and up to four AIM-7F Sparrow missiles if required. However, an AN/ALQ-119, AN/ALQ-131 or AN/ALQ-184 ECM pod was usually hung in the left forward Sparrow well and 'tuned' prior to a mission, so two rear-mounted AIM-7Fs were uploaded and Sidewinders gave way to HARMs. Selection of HARMs was flexible, as Lt Col Edward Ballanco explained;

'The firing sequence was normally the pilot's choice, but if you selected multiple stations, I believe they fired from left to right. Early on we had a problem with hand-off to the second missile, so we recommended selecting one station at a time after that. After three compressor stalls caused by the rocket blast, I was very particular about pulling the engine power back on the side of the missile being fired. Firing could be activated from either cockpit.'

Maj Paul Gregory and Capt Vince Cooper experienced the hand-off problem on the first daylight mission of *Desert Storm*. They selected both missile stations and, after firing the left-hand missile from their pair, they found that the other HARM had failed. On return it was found that the firing signal had gone to both missiles at once, and the second one had burned out on its pylon.

The 600-gallon F-15-type Royal Jet centreline fuel tank was chosen by McDonnell Douglas, as it could be flown when full or partially empty without the 'g' constraints of the original 600-gallon type. Underwing tanks were usually carried too, at the expense of weapons on the outboard pylons. One disadvantage of the tanks in the early years was that the aircraft's fuel system only indicated whether they were full or empty, making fuel and range calculations in flight difficult.

A pair of 561st TFS/35th TFW F-4Gs laden with AGM-78D Standard ARMs and single 600-gallon F-15-type Royal Jet centreline fuel tanks wait for 70th TFS/347th TFW F-4Es from Moody AFB, Georgia, to fill up before continuing a hunter-killer training sortie in the early 1980s. Their interim low visibility markings pre-date the move to wrap-around camouflage (*USAF*)

WEASELS, EAST AND WEST

F-4G training began at George AFB in 1978, with some veteran 'weaselers' bringing Vietnam experience to the courses. B-52 flight simulators were used for EWO ground training. Some trainees from George AFB's courses remained on base with the 561st or 562nd TFSs, but others were posted to the 81st TFS in USAFE, where the F-4Gs took over from the well-worn F-4Cwws. Others went to the 90th TFS at Clark AFB in the Philippines, where F-4Gs joined the squadron's complement of F-4Es from 30 July 1979. Wearing large 'weasel mouth' markings to distinguish them from the sharksmouths applied to the F-4Es of the base's 3rd TFW, they flew hunter-killer sorties in which the *Weasels* would supply air-defence targets for pairs of Phantom IIs to attack.

The 90th TFS had to face a real confrontation with North Korea on 26 August 1971 when SR-71A 64-17976, flown by Maj Maury Rosenberg and Capt E D McKim of the 9th Strategic Reconnaissance Wing's Kadena-based Detachment 1, repeatedly overflew Choc Tarrie island at the western end of the Korean Demilitarized Zone (DMZ). Their mission was to check on the construction of a suspected SA-2 site, but it had become active sooner than expected. The crew received a launch warning, and Maury saw a smoke trail heading directly for them, accelerating to Mach 3.2. He turned further into South Korean airspace and saw the SA-2 explode at 80,000 ft two miles behind them. Clark's F-4Gs were called in to fly SEAD sorties along the DMZ for future SR-71 missions, and there was no further SAM activity from North Korea.

Weasel crews from Clark AB could participate in the regular *Cope Thunder* training exercises that began in 1976, and they continued to provide combat-type experience to pilots from the Pacific Rim countries until the enforced closure of Clark AB in 1992.

The 90th TFS/3rd TFW began to receive F-4Gs in July 1979 at Clark AB, in the Philippines, operating 12 together with F-4Es until May 1991 when the Wing had to move to Elmendorf AFB, Alaska. Newly converted F-4G-42-MC 69-0283 was amongst the *Weasels* sent to the 90th TFS, the aircraft having previously spent almost two years on loan to the Imperial Iranian Air Force in the early 1970s. Photographed during a training sortie in 1980, the jet was written off in an accident at Clark AB on 12 January 1981 (*USAF*)

'Gs' FOR GERMANY

The first USAFE F-4G (69-0273) arrived for the 52nd TFW at Spangdahlem AB on 28 March 1983, flown by the commander of the resident 81st TFS, Lt Col 'Duke' Green – F-4Gs were often manned by crews with long experience of the Phantom II who had a real affection for the aircraft. The unit's base was just ten minutes' flying time from the Fulda Gap, the anticipated corridor for any sudden Soviet crossing of the River Rhine and incursion into NATO territory.

The 81st's routines included great emphasis on 'crew coordination items' that enabled them to work as a team. Pilots from single-seat fighters who were somewhat reluctant to share their command of an aircraft soon came to respect the knowledge and skill of their EWOs, many of whom could identify an emitting radar signal on the RWR within seconds. The F-4Gs initially flew as single aircraft in a hunter-killer team with a pair of F-4Es, and the squadron composition was eight F-4Gs and 16 F-4Es. By 1986 the unit was also operating with the EF-111A Ravens of the 42nd Electronic Combat Squadron at RAF Upper Heyford, in Oxfordshire, under the auspices of the 65th Air Division.

Unlike F-4G crews flying in *Desert Storm*, the sorties undertaken by the 81st FS were usually flown at low altitude to defeat SAMs. The 'Fan Song' radar had a blind spot (or 'notch') in separating a target aircraft from ground 'clutter' at low altitude, although later SAMs with faster-acting radar systems were more capable in that respect. They could track an aircraft's velocity and also be launched visually at low-flying targets. The low-altitude USAF camouflage paint scheme that had proven effective in Vietnam was therefore retained, and later replaced in the late 1970s by the even duller 'wrap-around' Euro 1 'slime and sludge' scheme of greens and grey with low-visibility markings.

USAFE practice missions involved approaching a target area at very low altitude and high speed, using terrain masking where possible and 'popping up' at times to update the AN/APR-38 on the threat situation. For a Shrike launch, the pilot advanced within range of the missile, pulled up in a 4.5g climb, rolled inverted, launched and then rolled upright to egress or make a further attack with 'iron' bombs or CBUs on the assumption that the site would have been damaged or shut down. Shrike's short range meant

that this procedure had to be completed very rapidly, making the HARM an essential replacement weapon, with a possible follow-up attack by a stand-off AGM-65D Maverick missile.

Weasels in USAFE faced a new generation of Soviet anti-aircraft missiles from the late 1960s starting with the SA-6 'Gainful' and its 'Straight Flush' radar, using semi-active radar homing. With three missiles per launcher unit, each SA-6 was guided by 'Straight Flush' until in final phase of the interception, when the weapon used its own internal radar to lock on to the target and destroy it. Capable of 'pulling' 15g in a turn 'Gainful' could be impossible to avoid.

From 1972, Soviet ground forces also fielded the SA-8 'Gecko' (9k-33 'Osa') and SA-9 'Gaskin' mobile SAM systems. 'Gecko's' 9A-33 all-terrain transporter-erector vehicle carried six missiles and its own radar, and being highly mobile it could accompany armoured ground forces and remain hard to detect from the air. Although the SA-8 had a fairly short range of around six miles, the system could detect and fire at an aircraft within seconds, making evasion extremely difficult and giving an F-4G EWO even more threats to manage. At low altitudes, pilots also faced an increasing range of IR-guided MANPADS that could not be detected in advance and were defeated only by flares or violent manoeuvring. Pilots had no IR warning system aboard the F-4G.

The overwhelming numbers of Soviet armoured and air defence units led to the force-multiplying use of hunter-killer teams, similar in purpose to the original F-100 and F-105 teams of the 1960s, but employing far more sophisticated F-4G and F-4E Phantom II (later replaced by F-16CJs) aircraft. The 52nd TFW's 23rd TFS became a unique unit through its use of both types of aircraft for this team mission.

Weasel crews had to maintain their proficiency levels or 'currencies' with training sorties from their home base (weather permitting) and through short deployments abroad to use the Spadeadam range in England, to Sardinia for regular air-to-air training and through six-monthly visits to Zaragoza, in Spain, for 30-day weapons training detachments on the Bardenas bombing range. Like other pilots, their 'mission qualified' status was maintained through specific numbers of flight hours, weapons delivery

F-4G-42-MC 69-0286 in full 81st TFS/ 52nd TFW regalia, including the *Wild Weasel IV* squadron patch and yellow fin tip. Crews flying this aircraft were credited with six SAM site kills during *Desert Storm* (*T.Panopalis Collection*)

The green and grey Euro I colour scheme emphasised the F-4G's pugilistic appearance. F-4G-42-MC 69-0251's wrap-around camouflage was relieved by a drop-shadowed base code. The cool, dark safety of a USAFE hardened aircraft shelter in West Germany was in stark contrast to the open-air, baking hot conditions that the aircraft would experience in Bahrain from August 1990 (*T Panopalis Collection*)

sorties and night operations, as well as the regular employment of their specialised anti-radar skills.

Training sorties were not always focused entirely on the *Weasel* role, as 52nd TFW F-4G EWO Col William 'Budman' Redmond recalled;

'The toughest thing [when training] was avoiding no-fly zones – there seemed to be a million of them. What was fun was the Rules of Engagement that allowed for anybody to "jump" anybody else, so it made low-level [flying] and an operating area a fun time. I probably spent about 60 per cent of my time [with my eyes] out of the cockpit, 30 per cent on the air-to-air radar and ten per cent using the *Weasel* equipment.'

Very detailed 90-minute preparation for a four-ship sortie occurred in the squadron briefing room ('The Vault'), and included the latest intelligence information on the location of SAM systems and AAA along the Iron Curtain borders. For practice attacks on range targets, the briefing focused on details of the strike package that the *Weasels* would support, routes to and from the target, timing, relevant callsigns and use of countermeasures. Communication was via *Have Quick* radios, which changed frequencies daily and used secure coded frequency sequences.

FALCONS AND *WEASELS*

Replacement of Spangdahlem's F-4Es was a complex process. Col Jim Uken explained the background to the F-16's original adoption;

'We [at Spangdahlem] were notified in late 1986 that the F-4Es were being replaced by F-16Cs that were originally destined for Ramstein AB to replace the F-4Es there. This was because the Pentagon "suddenly" realised that Spangdahlem's F-4Es would start transferring to the Turkish air force in the fall of 1987 – a sale agreed before the decision was made to convert Spangdahlem to mixed F-4E/G units in 1983.

'The F-4G/F-16C mix was intended as an interim solution until the next *Wild Weasel* platform was selected and in production. To that end, the USAF had signed a Statement of Need stipulating the capabilities required in the Follow-on *Wild Weasel* (FoWW), which included an existing, in-production two-seat fighter capable of four-HARM employment, the ability to swap over and use the F-4G's EW suites, antennas, etc., and a host of flight characteristics like speed, high-g [limits] and combat ceiling and radius.

'In less than a year three contenders submitted bids – McDonnell Douglas proposed the F-15G, Panavia the ECR Tornado and General Dynamics the F-16G, although the latter did not qualify based on a two-HARM employment capability only and failure to meet some of the flight characteristics. McDonnell Douglas was so confident that it would win that it even converted an F-15 simulator in St Louis to a fully functional F-15G front and rear cockpit, which I got a few hours' time in and have to admit that I really liked.'

Col William Redmond was also impressed by the simulator;

'I thought it was great. I went on to fly the F-15E, and its sensor suites plus the AN/APR-47 would have made a great follow-on to the F-4G. Its weaponry, manoeuvrability and fuel capacity would have given it airframe advantages. The ability to move the *Wild Weasel* data between up to four different display screens would have been a great advantage when it came to seeing the threat picture.'

Col Redmond later commanded the 4th FW's 336th FS, flying F-15E Strike Eagles from Seymour Johnson AFB, in North Carolina.

Development work on the integration of F-4G and F-16C tactics was conducted by crews from Detachment 5 of the 4485th Test and Evaluation Squadron (TES). Amongst the personnel involved was (then) Maj Uken, who recalled;

'Little did we know that at the time politics concerning the future of the *Wild Weasel* were already underway at upper echelons in the Pentagon. So, on 12 January 1987, Capt Scott Anderson and I flew an F-4G to Luke AFB, Arizona, to meet up with two F-16Cs from the 4485th TES and start our Test Design and Evaluation work on how best to use the F-16 as a *Wild Weasel* wingman.

'Prior to our first Barry M Goldwater Range mission to use their threat emitters, we got our first surprise. It turned out that the F-16's weapons computer did not have a Weapons ID for the AGM-45 Shrike, as it was never intended to carry or fire the missile. This was easily resolved by "lying" to the F-16's computer, telling it that an AGM-45 was on its [launch] rail and giving it a direct fire impulse to the Shrike.

'Over the next four days we flew six sorties with the two F-16s, starting with formation work and quickly moving into teaching the F-16 pilots Shrike employment techniques. The last two or three sorties focused on data transfer techniques and trying to get their eyes on the emitter targets for simulated free-fall ordnance employment, such as Mk 82 500-lb bombs.

The AGM-65A/B Maverick and its 215-lb warhead could be guided from its LAU-117/A launcher exactly to a target by its electro-optical contrast-seeking TV guidance system in conditions of good visibility. The AGM-65D, which entered service in 1986 and was used by F-4G units, had an imaging IR seeker, which was particularly useful for homing onto heat sources in low-visibility conditions, and a 220-lb blast-fragmentation warhead (*USAF*)

'On 23 January [1987], Scott and I took an F-4G to Bergstrom AFB, Texas, to use the Fort Hood Range complex with the same two F-16 pilots, flying another eight missions over a four-day period. The focus this time was on exploring even more data transfer methods for the F-16s, and even trying to "sensor cue" inert AGM-65 IR-guided Mavericks against actual operating threat emitters. The hope was that, with the pilot following his steering cues while continuing to close in on the emitter within the "field of view" of the Maverick's seeker head, the heat from the emitting antenna and its attached generators or the engines from mobile emitter vehicles would eventually reveal the target's location.

'Ultimately, the "sensor cue" trials met with limited success for a number of reasons, including accuracy of data transfer, INS platform "drift" over time and the elevation of the emitters at ground level – the lower you were flying, the more critical any elevation error would be. Whereas the F-4G continued to update and refine information on an emitter's location until actual weapon release, the further out the emitter location was from where the data was transferred to the F-16 transfer point, the more error was induced. A three-degree error at 15 nautical miles translated into a distance of 4500 ft – good enough for anti-radiation missiles against a radiating emitter, but pretty bad when trying to find a camouflaged target.

'Over a three-week span in late March/early April that year the 4485th brought two F-16Cs and one F-16D, with four pilots, to George AFB, where we flew a "two x two" schedule almost every day using two of our test-configured F-4Gs with their F-16s. We used radar emitters at the Nellis range complex, or at the US Navy's China Lake range, expanding the number of test crews involved. My log shows 18 sorties over that period, with the goal of being able to brief the headquarters of the Tactical Air Warfare Center on our results and, thereby, the leadership at Spangdahlem and the Fighter Weapons School graduates there before the F-16Cs arrived.'

Maj Uken and a group of Detachment 5 electronics experts also had the chance to test the newest Operational Flight Test (OFP 6000) software in an F-4G in the European electronic signal environment 'to see if we discovered any surprises. We loaded this "tape" into a line 52nd TFW F-4G and I flew with the Chief of Wing Weapons and squadron pilots. Highlights included being able to work with radars like the Rapier, German Gepard, Bloodhound, I-HAWK, Patriot and – in a very "hush-hush" mission in the far north in the West German buffer zone – an East German SA-5 "Gammon" SAM at Rostock that "might just be doing some radar testing at a particular time".

'For a couple of missions we obtained permission to take a Spangdahlem F-4G to RAF Coningsby to fly with RAF test crews for the Phantom FGR 2 and the ADV Tornado with the newest Foxhunter radar. On the latter, where we were flying over The Wash, the Tornado crew ran through all of the operating modes to see if we had any classification anomalies when we switched modes from one to another. I was debriefing them on one of the many runs, and I had noted that in one case our RHAW gear [AN/APR-47] seemed to be having a hard time deciding if the operating frequency was 9xx5 or 9xx6 MHz. The Tornado pilot took a booklet out of his flightsuit leg pocket, flipped over a few pages, stopped and showed it to his navigator. He then said to me, "That must be one bloody amazing piece of kit.

The frequency is classified, of course, but it is actually 9xx5.5 MHz".'

By 1990, the introduction of F-16C Block 30 aircraft into all three 52nd TFW squadrons gave the 23rd, 81st and 480th TFSs 12 F-4Gs and 12 F-16CJs each to fly hunter-killer missions with. Col Kurt Dittmer was involved in the initiation of that partnership;

'When USAFE announced the replacement of the F-4Es with F-16s, "Uke" [Jim Uken] and I were involved in stating the requirements for, and the testing

The F-4G and F-16CJ 'colour jets' of the 52nd TFW fly in close formation for the benefit of a USAFE photographer during a flight from Spangdahlem over the Eifel region in December 1987. The first examples of the Wild Weasel-optimised F-16 had reached the 52nd just a matter of months before this shot was taken. Each of the Wing's three squadrons had 12 F-4Gs and 12 F-16CJs to fly hunter-killer missions with by 1990 (*USAF*)

of, the F-16 Aircraft Launcher Interface Computer (ALIC) that initially used the Maverick missile circuits to launch a Shrike and, later, a HARM. Using the ALIC with a Shrike, the mixed force tactics were very similar to targeting an F-4E carrying a Shrike. The F-16 used an LAU-88 [Hughes LAU-88/A triple-rail launcher for the AGM-65 Maverick missile] for the Shrike, as all it needed was a "fire" impulse and not the AGM-65 "video" interface that the ALIC used.

'The [F-16] pilot had no control over the Shrike, except in selecting which one was fired if you carried a mixed load [pre-programmed] for different frequency ranges. ALIC could use the LAU-88/A video interface to allow the pilot to use the Maverick switchology in his cockpit to access computer pages, selecting items on the menu by slewing, and then designating the item or page he wanted to access.

'An F-4G could also pass information to a HARM on an F-16 for the launch so that it would fly to the correct altitude for its flight profile. When interfacing with an F-4G, the F-16-mounted HARM did not get aircraft information from its ALIC, so a 2.5-degree climb was all we needed, as well as being "wings level", for the shot, as this was the flight condition sent from the F-4G to the HARM. The F-4G EWO would radio the SAM type, heading and range to the Viper pilot, select the HARM, slew the cursor to "RK" ["Radar Kill"], select the SAM type and then turn the jets to the correct heading for the shoot. We now had a chance of returning to our wives if we went to war. Yay!'

Dittmer emphasised that pulling up to a 45-degree nose-high position 12 miles from a SAM site 'put you in the heart of the ZSU-23-4 anti-aircraft guns, which was not survivable. We were like skeet to the ZSUs!'

Pairing the F-16C up with the F-4G added to the latter type's wider threat detection and warning ability, and also emphasised the superior flexibility of HARM. The F-16C's AN/APG-66 digital radar, optimised for air-to-air modes, also gave the pair superior protection from aerial threats. Target information from the F-4G could be passed via ALIC to HARM rounds if the F-16C was carrying them so that they could be re-programmed to attack newly detected threats. In combat, mission planning had to allow for the F-4G's higher fuel consumption and shorter time on station than the F-16C.

CHAPTER FOUR

'BIG GEORGE'

F-4G-44-MC 69-7561 of the 561st TFS/ 37th TFW leads an F-4E from the same squadron in a banking turn over the flightline at George AFB in August 1984. The F-4E is carrying inert HARM training rounds, while the *Weasel* also has solitary inert AGM-45 Shrike, AGM-65 Maverick and AGM-78 Standard ARM rounds on its underwing pylons (*USAF*)

The 39th Tactical Fighter Training Squadron (TFTS) received the first production F-4G-42-MC (69-0239) on 28 April 1978 at George AFB, which was to be the *Wild Weasels'* home. It had operated various F-4 Phantom II versions since the spring of 1964, initially with the seven squadrons of the 479th TFW and, from October 1971, with the 35th TFW. The latter wing flew every USAF fighter version of the F-4, trained Luftwaffe F-4F crews and included both F-4Cwws and F-4Gs within its 21st and 39th TFTSs. The F-4Gs were shared between both units, and *Weasel* pilots were required to undertake the same classroom courses as their EWOs so that they would be familiar with the threat systems they would face and the back-seaters' methods of combating them. Dealing with mobile SAM launchers was a priority when learning how to use the AN/APR-38 and -47 systems.

All assets of the 39th TFTS were transferred to the 562nd TFS, a former F-105 unit, on 9 October 1980. That same year, the 561st TFS commenced flying F-4Gs, while retaining some F-4Es. The massive base also accommodated the 37th TFW, which took over the *Wild Weasel* training task from March 1981 and developed new hunter-killer tactics using F-4Gs and F-4Es. The introduction of the F-117A Nighthawk in 1989 took the 37th TFW to Tonopah, in Nevada, to take over the 4450th Tactical Group, manage the introduction of the 'stealth fighter' and train its pilots (known as 'Bandits').

The F-4Gs, now operated by the 561st and 562nd TFSs, together with the 563rd TFS (which had become operational as an F-4G unit in January 1979 and been assigned to the 37th TFW in March 1981) returned to 35th TFW control at that point until the closure of George AFB in December 1992.

George was also home to Detachment 5 of the 4485th TES from the USAF's Tactical Air Warfare Centre at Eglin AFB. The detachment specialised in development of the F-4G, and it used three aircraft, initially pooled with the 562nd TFS, until it was re-located to Nellis AFB as Detachment 6. It was responsible for all aspects of test and evaluation for the F-4G and its weapons systems, including HARM updates, trialling low-cost HARM seeker heads and testing the aircraft's new digital fuel gauge. Detachment 5 was also responsible for the adoption of the Hill Gray colour scheme, which F-4Gs and RF-4Cs wore in the Gulf conflict. Maj Uken participated in the scheme change;

'I was at Det 5 and involved in the impetus to get the grey-on-grey scheme. In 1983–84, we were still flying with Vietnam-camouflaged F-4Es, which were thought to be survivable at low level in USAFE. Then at Det 5 we tested the greys vs the Euro 1 scheme [dark greens and grey] and decided that the grey was less visible in the vast majority of situations. The Air Force decided to do all the F-4Gs in grey, chosen initially because it was more suitable for the European scenario. In Operation *Desert Storm*, the high-altitude mission was needed for fuel [economy] reasons and because of AAA, and the hazy conditions made the grey scheme more suitable.'

At the start of Operation *Desert Shield* in August 1990, at least one Shaikh Isa-based F-4G still had its Euro 1 camouflage scheme.

The 37th TFW's 'colour jet' leads the COs' aircraft from the 561st, 562nd and 563rd TFSs during a photo-exercise from George AFB in 1987. All the F-4Gs are carrying inert HARM training rounds. The jet closest to the camera is F-4G-42-MC 69-0281, which served with the 563rd from 1986–89. Sent to AMARC in June 1992, it was converted into a QF-4G and destroyed in a missile test in May 2002 (*USAF*)

A Texas Instruments AGM-45 Shrike leaves the pylon of 561st TFS F-4G-43-MC 69-7231 and begins to climb to the altitude from which the missile will identify its target and dive towards it. Shrike did not require the specialised *Wild Weasel* weapons control systems that made HARM a more effective missile, and it could be carried by several types of aircraft. Shrike equipped *Wild Weasels* from March 1966 and remained in service until the early 1990s (*USAF*)

TO THE DESERT

By August 1990, when Iraqi forces invaded Kuwait, the F-4G units were well practised in their craft. They would clearly be vital in penetrating Iraq's elaborate, modern integrated air defence systems (IADS). Its command-and-control network, covering much of Iraq, was based on the sophisticated French KARI (Iraq in French, but reversed) system, masterminded by the Ericsson Company, which linked more than 150 SAM and AAA batteries. Iraq operated eight types of Russian SAM, together with French Rolands, totalling more than 16,000 missiles, and around 10,000 AAA weapons. Having grabbed Kuwait, Saddam also had access to a number of American-made MIM-23B HAWK SAMs. Coalition forces would defeat KARI partly by mounting attacks involving hundreds of aircraft, rather than the small packages of up to 20 that KARI was designed to handle.

The initial Coalition forces' response to the Iraq invasion was Operation *Desert Shield*, which was mounted essentially to protect the vulnerable Saudi Arabian oilfields from similar incursion to the one that had befallen neighbouring Kuwait. Initially, two squadrons of F-15C Eagles from Col John McBroom's 1st TFW left Langley AFB, Virginia, to be based at Dhahran, in Saudi Arabia, on 7 August. George AFB began deploying 561st TFS F-4Gs to the newly constructed Shaikh Isa AB in Bahrain five days later, the unit being led by its new squadron commander, Lt Col George Walton. The *Wild Weasels'* original destination was to have been Dubai, but the F-15E Strike Eagle component was diverted there from Oman. The F-4Gs initially forward-deployed to Seymour Johnson AFB while the basing situation in Bahrain was sorted out.

Each F-4G in the four cells of six aircraft was loaded for the transit flight with three external fuel tanks, a pair of HARMs and three AIM-7F Sparrows for self-defence against fighters of the Iraqi Air Force (IrAF). They headed off in the dark to a destination for which Lt Col Walton had only a satellite reconnaissance photograph for guidance, and plans for multiple KC-10 aerial refuelling link-ups en route at around 360 mph over the Atlantic and Red Sea that would give each Phantom II 21 'plugs' for fuel during the 15.6 hrs non-stop flight. Four jets had to divert en route with problems, two spending eight days at Lajes, in the Azores.

Diplomatic clearance to land in Bahrain was only established during the flight. On arrival, crews found a newly built base with no fuel storage tanks and only one refuelling truck. Sandbags were used in the absence of parking chocks. The maintenance crews who arrived a day later had to sleep under the wings of the aircraft, or in a hangar, for the first three nights. All maintenance was done in the open, with personnel exposed to extremely high temperatures. There was a main 13,000 ft runway and a single taxiway, but no proper parking ramps for the Phantom IIs and the Royal Bahraini Air Force's own F-5E/F Tigers and F-16s.

The F-4Gs were soon joined by a large US Marine Corps force comprising 3rd Marine Air Wing F/A-18 Hornets, AV-8B Harrier IIs and A-6E Intruders on a base designed for 800 personnel. Later, RF-4C Phantom IIs from the 192nd Tactical Reconnaissance Squadron (TRS) of the Nevada ANG and the 12th TRS from Bergstrom AFB, Texas, added to the crush.

Officers at Shaikh Isa were crowded into huts with corrugated iron roofs and bunks that had to be shared between pilots on day and night missions on the 'hot bunking' rota. The main social comfort from November 1990 was the privately-run 'Weasel Dome', a pressurised tent where food and (unusually) beer were available during the *Desert Shield* phase as slight relief from the painfully overcrowded accommodation on base.

Exploratory missions near Kuwait began on 21 August, and ELINT flights collected signals from the Iraqi defence systems. When *Desert Storm* commenced, the 12th TRS took advantage of locally available *Weasel* protection. Col Uken remembered that 'they would check our flying schedule and quite often align their take-off times with F-4G sorties'.

F-4G-44-MC 69-7574 marked as the 35th TFW flagship at George AFB in early 1990 just months prior to the aircraft being deployed to Shaikh Isa AB in August of that year. The yellow fin cap stripe represents the 561st TFS and blue was the 562nd TFTS *Weasels* colour. The Wing's two F-4E training squadrons, the 20th and 21st TFTSs are represented by silver and black, respectively (*Author's Collection*)

Planning for the relief of Kuwait in *Desert Storm* began early on in *Desert Shield*. Former *Wild Weasel* pilot Lt Gen 'Chuck' Horner led a team including Brig Lt Gen Larry Henry (a *Weasel* wing commander) that designed a complex air campaign to free Kuwait, defend Saudi Arabia and reduce Iraq's military capability. The result was a 600-page Air Tasking Order (ATO) that gave details of every aerial sortie to be flown by aircraft of the coalition of nations which had been assembled to achieve the objectives of the Tactical Air Control Centre, established at Riyadh, in Saudi Arabia. It reflected months of close study and analysis of every aspect of the defences, largely without the aid of computers which arrived much later. At first, ATOs were delivered to the squadrons by a C-21A Learjet rather than via the planning cells' single fax machine.

Foremost among those aims was the neutralisation of Iraqi IADS, specifically the comprehensive SAM network and the IrAF. All of the latter were controlled from four sector operations centres, three covering the north, central area and south of Iraq, and one for Kuwait. All were answerable to a central headquarters in Baghdad.

Within the ATO, the 81st TFS was mainly tasked for missions over Kuwait, while the 561st TFS focused on the Baghdad area. Both units would also protect strike forces hitting Iraq's numerous airfields, and after the third day, the allocation of missions was more fluid and ATOs became more flexible.

SAM suppression was seen as a vital part of the campaign from the outset, particularly by the US Navy and US Marine Corps contingents. A team led by Brig Gen Larry Henry devised strategies to make the best use of its F-4Gs, EF-111A Raven jammers and EC-130 *Compass Call* communications monitoring aircraft in conjunction with the SEAD-wielding US Navy and US Marine Corps EA-6B Prowlers and F/A-18 Hornets. They would protect bomber F-16 formations of up to 20 aircraft, with F-15C Eagle fighter escorts.

Increasingly through *Desert Shield*, these aircraft were used in large force employments that approached the borders between Saudi Arabia, Kuwait

81st TFS pilots and WSOs, complete with essential headgear and shades, line up at Shaikh Isa. Parked behind them is F-4G-45-MC 69-7587, which was credited with destroying five SAM sites during *Desert Storm* (*Lt Col Ed Ballanco Collection*)

and Iraq in an openly provocative way to explore the enemy's air defence capability and provide aircrews with pre-combat experience. Composite Force Training formations testing similar tactics included flights from other air forces such as Qatar's. The intensity of these excursions and the size of the formations increased steadily into December 1990 while there was still hope that Iraqi dictator President Saddam Hussein could be persuaded to pull his forces out of Kuwait.

Weasel F-4Gs usually mounted two flights per day throughout the week, apart from the Muslim holy day on Friday to avoid offending the local population. Training for the 561st FS contingent included the practice of using the same crews in the same four-ship formations for virtually all missions so that they developed close rapport that would prove invaluable in combat. As Col Uken explained, 'About half the sorties were at night. If a crew started on a night rotation they spent the majority of the war in that time slot'.

'SPANG' SUPPRESSORS

The hunter-killer concept, pairing F-4Gs and F-16Cs, was abandoned at Shaikh Isa in favour of using only Spangdahlem's 52nd TFW F-4Gs when its 81st TFS was also deployed, with little warning, on an eight-hour flight to Bahrain from 5 September. Like the unit's George-based predecessors, it had little specific preparation for the new basing and few crews had experience of live-firing costly HARMs.

Another 12 F-4Gs from the 52nd TFW were flown to Shaikh Isa on 26 December 1990 as 'battle loss replacements' for the 81st TFS, although mercifully there had been no losses to enemy defences up to that point in *Desert Shield*. As Col Uken recalled, they were a mixed batch of F-4Gs;

'When we got the Warning Order that we were about to deploy, the 52nd TFW pulled jets from all three squadrons at "Spang" to get those with the most hours available until the next phase inspection and overhaul was due. Amongst the aircraft sent was F-4G 69-7232, which had been a 480th TFS "red tail" in the initial deployment in early September. When the 81st TFS became re-flagged as a 24-strong F-4G Unit Equipped squadron on 1 January 1991, the remaining 12 F-4Gs that had arrived at Shaikh Isa on 26 December were assigned to the 81st TFS. After the re-alignment of the new 81st TFS and "hard crewing" of eight four-ship flights, we immediately began training as such. On average, each four-ship completed seven or eight sorties flying as an element prior to the *Desert Storm* kick-off.'

Aerial refuelling was a massive undertaking throughout *Desert Storm*, involving nine provisional wings of KC-135s positioned throughout the area and around 30 KC-10As which supplied aircraft on long deployments to the theatre (during *Desert Shield*), as well as those on combat missions. The pilot of this F-4G from the 81st TFS appears to have raised his seat to see past the canopy bow for a better view of the tanker's formation indicator markings so that he can maintain the correct position (*Lt Col Ed Ballanco Collection*)

Lt Gen Buster C Glosson was made Director of Air Campaign Plans in Riyadh in August 1990. A former Vietnam War F-4 pilot, he was insistent on the USAF allowing him to use its most sophisticated combat assets in *Desert Storm*, including the E-8 Joint Surveillance Target Attack Radar System aircraft and the F-15E Strike Eagle, for the air operation. Key members of the planning team for tackling Iraq's IADS included Lt Col Jim Keck from the 562nd TFS and Lt Col Ed Ballanco, who brought long experience of the SEAD business and the F-4G. As the latter explained;

'I was the wing weapons officer, and as such the primary planner for *Desert Storm* [which was] a top-secret plan and ATO up until the day before execution. After I arrived on 5 September 1990, I went to Riyadh for a few days to work with the people in the "Black Hole". While there, we coordinated all the *Wild Weasel* missions with the unit representatives and planners. Initially, we worked the details on the first missions that were very complex. Of course, the thinking going into it was that *Desert Storm* would last for four days, with two weather backups.

'After my visit to Riyadh, I made several trips to meet the units and plan the missions face to face. Most of the trips were early on [October–November timeframe}. One trip was to Doha [in Qatar] to plan the mission with [Lt Col Bruce] "Orville" Wright, my first UPT [Undergraduate Pilot Training] student, so we had been friends for a long time. Orville had also been a *Wild Weasel*, so he knew the mission. Since my Wing was going to support this mission, I took a particular interest in it. As the forces were "plussed up", beginning in November, we did most of the coordination using the ATO updates. Many of the missions expanded after that time, but the basic plan remained essentially the same.'

As the 52nd TFW's head of weapons and tactics, Lt Col Ballanco had pioneered the use of teamwork by F-4Gs and F-16Cs with EF-111A Ravens and EC-130s to combat Soviet air defences in a hypothetical invasion of Central Europe. One of his recommendations was that F-4Gs should operate at altitudes above 20,000 ft, rather than dodging hostile search radars and SAMs by flying at minimal heights as they did in Vietnam, thereby becoming vulnerable to a plethora of AAA.

OPENING MOVES

Five months after the first 561st TFS *Weasels* arrived in Saudi Arabia, the orders for H-Hour – the beginning of hostilities – were finally issued. In the first Task Force *Normandy* attack launched by the Coalition as part of *Desert Storm*, US Army AH-64A Apaches from the 101st Airborne Division and USAF MH-53J *Pave Low* helicopters took out two P-15M(2) 'Squat Eye' and 'Flat Face' C-band target acquisition radars and 'Spoon Rest' A-band radars on the Saudi–Iraqi border. This created a safe corridor up to eight miles wide near Ma'anya for the F-15E strike aircraft and EF-111A Ravens to pass through and hit Scud missile locations on H-2 and H-3 airfields in western Iraq.

The opening action of Operation *Desert Storm* on 17 January 1991 involved more than 2000 aircraft. F-4Gs and EF-111As would lead F-15Es, F-111Fs, F-16Cs and other strike aircraft on missions against IADS targets and the four 'species' of SS-1 Scud missiles that were capable of delivering chemical or biological warheads from fixed or mobile locations. The EF-111As could jam radars over a wide area, while the F-4Gs had to attack them one at a time. In addition, more than 100 Brunswick ADM-141 tactical air-launched drones crisscrossed Kuwait and southern Iraq after being launched by Coalition jets. Simulating combat aircraft, they forced Iraqi radar operators to power up their equipment and thereby become targets for SEAD aircraft.

As another prelude to the first wave of attacks, 44 BQM-74C Chukar weapons target training drones were also launched into Iraq, imitating strike aircraft and 'bringing up' more air defence radars for the *Weasels* to attack. Amongst the jets involved in the early wave of missions were F-117A Nighthawks of the 415th TFS, which attacked command and control centres around Baghdad, evading the KARI systems. The power supply for the IADS was also targeted. SEAD missions against ground defences were flown by a wide variety of aircraft including HARM-carrying US Marine Corps F/A-18s, as well as the dedicated F-4Gs, EA-6B Prowlers and EF-111As, in a far-reaching campaign to eliminate Iraq's supposedly impregnable defences.

Maj Jim Uken was amongst the *Wild Weasel* crews primed for action that first night;

'On the afternoon prior to the first night, a brigadier general from the CENTCOM [US Central Command] Air Staff arrived from Riyadh and all aircrew were assembled for a briefing, where the "Gentlemen, tonight we ride" message was given. Although it was supposed to be kept top secret, most of the maintenance personnel had figured out that tonight would be the night. Some enterprising crew chiefs had even planted a US flag atop the last revetment on the flightline, with a light illuminating a banner beneath it. I was later told that virtually every crewman saluted as they taxied by.

'As the 561st TFS had arrived in-theatre first, and all F-4s were under Operational Control of the 35th TFW(Provisional), the 561st was selected to spearhead the opening Baghdad strikes while the 81st TFS was sent to Kuwait and southeastern Iraq. Accordingly, the majority of the 561st jets were loaded with two HARMs and three external tanks, while most 81st TFS jets carried four HARMs and one external tank due to the shorter

distances involved and the large number of SAMs they expected to be shot at them.'

Preceding that first wave of manned aircraft into Kuwait at two minutes prior to 'H-hour' was a flight of four F-4Gs led by 69-7232 'Pearl 51', with 81st TFS CO Lt Col Randy Gelwix at the controls and WSO Maj Uken in the rear cockpit. The latter explained;

'As we were going "across the fence" first into Kuwait, we were also the first to take off. I was struck immediately by how combat operations would change a lot of things. For example, instead of having ten to 20 waypoints programmed into our INS, my first steer point was to the air refuelling track rendezvous point, the next was the Kuwait border crossing point and the third our middle-of-Kuwait internal steer point. Also, next to no communications were going on so the radios were strangely quiet. Although there wasn't much radio chatter, one look at the radar told you that there were hundreds of aircraft out there. I believe there were more than 2000 Coalition aircraft involved in the first night. In certain respects, it's somewhat amazing that there were no mid-air collisions.

'Our four-ship arrived at the refuelling track and got the necessary fuel top-off prior to heading north. There were refuelling tracks stretching from the Persian Gulf all the way across northern Saudi Arabia to the Red Sea. Each track was aligned north-to-south, with "anchors" [contact points] separated by 50 nautical miles. Refuelling altitudes were between flight levels 180–280 (1800–2800 ft), with most of the tracks having between two and five tankers operating at different even altitudes within the track.

'According to the ATO, we were the first manned Coalition aircraft to enter Iraqi-controlled airspace at two minutes before H-hour. The INS said "you are now in Kuwait", and I was thinking "how can they not see us coming?" I expected all hell to break loose, but nothing happened. Shortly thereafter, however, it was almost like they knew when H-hour was because at that moment an SA-2 came up directly underneath our four-ship and, since we were flying a loose route formation, we all got the same "you are being launched at" indications. As we all went defensive at the same time, that was pretty much the last we saw of each other that night, but we had

The F-4G's front cockpit was very similar to the F-4E's, but with the addition of a plan position indicator and a radar warning and control panel. Major changes to the rear cockpit included rearrangement of the flight instruments along the top of the front panel, with three AN/APR-38/-47 displays below them. Beneath the edge of the radar scope (partially visible at top, centre) is the attitude direction indicator, flanked on the left by the airspeed and Mach gauges and the altimeter on the right. The attitude direction indicator has the angle-of-attack gauge and weapons selector panel to the lower left, with the master arm switch on a striped panel. Eight engine monitoring instruments are on the right-hand panel (*Author's Collection*)

On the pilot's immediate left are the twin engine throttles and engine start buttons (left), oxygen control panel, drag 'chute control handle (lower left) and the landing gear control, with its distinctive round-tipped handle. Other controls for fuel, the AN/ALE-40 countermeasures programmer and the pilot's g-suit are to the left of the throttles (*Author's Collection*)

briefed for every possible situation and just flexed to the plan.

'Our mission that night was to support simultaneous attacks on Iraqi-occupied airfields [Ali Al Salem, Al-Jabar and Kuwait International Airport] in Kuwait, defended by SA-2 and SA-3 SAMs and radar-guided AAA, as well as providing protection for ten US Marine Corps F/A-18s flying through central Iraq en route to their HARM launch points. In addition, there were three Iraqi Republican Guard [IRG] divisions on the Kuwait border with numerous SA-6s (we were briefed that they had 20 SA-6s each) and a lot of AAA. Operating in the middle of Kuwait, we were roughly mid-way between the three airfields and the SA-6s on the perimeter.

'"Pearl 2", "3" and "4" were each given an airfield of interest, usually defended by three SA-2s and SA-3s, with Gelwix and I flying as the "wild card" to flex as needed. Our configuration was four HARMs, two AIM-7s, an AN/ALQ-184 ECM pod, AN/ALE-40 chaff and flare dispensers and a Royal Jet centreline tank. Our four-ship expended 15 AGM-88 HARMs (I had one hang fire) in less than 15 minutes. The mission planners had foreseen that Kuwait might be hectic that first night, and fortunately had another four-ship of F-4Gs coming in 15 minutes behind us.'

Sixteen F-4Gs from the 81st TFS were assigned to the Kuwait theatre that first night, with eight additional F-4Gs from the 561st TFS, to support three large strike packages. The longer-ranging Baghdad missions by 16 F-4Gs from the 561st TFS, together with eight from the 81st TFS, required underwing drop tanks, reducing the jets' HARM load to two missiles per aircraft. Tanker support for all missions was vital, as some could involve flights of up to 3000 miles over vast desert terrain.

Weasel crews found that Iraqi radar operators were reluctant to stay on the air for more than a few seconds, and they shut down immediately if they realised that a *Weasel* had locked onto them. Little of the copious AAA around Baghdad appeared to be radar guided, and most of it only reached to around 15,000 ft. For the rest of the campaign the *Weasels* could concentrate on specific threats to strike aircraft packages.

Breaking with their normal USAFE operating altitudes of 2000–5000 ft, F-4G crews flew high both to avoid AAA and to maximise their range as their jets' J79 engines were far more fuel efficient above 20,000 ft than at lower levels. For the Kuwait mission, following Lt Col Ballanco's recommendation, this meant that they could replace their two external wing tanks with two extra HARMs. As he commented, 'This was a wonderful configuration, but we could not go very far or stay on station for very long. Also, we had to refuel to make it to Kuwait'. AAA remained a threat, however, and a desirable target for the F-4Gs. For Col Redmond, 'the only radar I really wanted to shoot was one guiding a ZSU-23-4 [four-barrelled 23 mm rapid-fire automatic gun unit], because I knew they were a helicopter threat for our Army brothers and sisters'.

Lt Col Ballanco had planned the first Kuwait Theatre of Operations (KTO) missions, and he flew on the second strike on 17 January. He decided to 'concentrate on the big picture, and leave the flying operations to the flight commanders, who were darn good!' Bellanco, therefore, took the No 6 slot in a six-ship flight, with Lt Col Don Whittler as his EWO in 'Coors 36';

'Although we were split into two different mission numbers, we had planned the ten-ship of *Wild Weasels* together as we had a wide time window to cover the full KTO. By planning together, we hoped to provide overlapping coverage in the event that anything went wrong. Because we were all carrying four HARMs each, there was a possibility that a flight might have excess missiles after covering the attack missions we were directly supporting. This would allow a transition from a Direct Support mission to an Area Support mission.

'We started our full mission briefing in the main briefing room that was known as the "church of what's happening now" because it was filled with church pew-type benches. The initial *Wild Weasel* flights were landing as we were briefing, so we did not receive any feedback from the crews, but we did know they had all made it back. This was an area of major concern because, while we were optimistic, we really did not know how well our systems would work against the air defences. The briefing was relatively uneventful, except that the weather was not as good as we had become accustomed to. There was a strong north wind and cumulus clouds throughout the area. During the briefing we had our first Scud alarm, and we all took cover under the benches. We later learned that the Scud alarm was triggered by explosions that our task force had created.

'When we arrived at the squadron duty desk to get our aircraft assignments, this was when things started going downhill. Of the six aircraft for "Coors" flight, only the two for "Coors 35" and "36" were ready. We were scheduled on different tankers but we were all supposed to enter the KTO at about the same time, with "Coors 31–34" supporting the attacks to the north and west [by F-16Cs of the South Carolina ANG's 169th TFW that were attacking SAM sites near the IRG area along the Kuwait–Iraq border] and "Coors 35" and "36" supporting the southeast area attacks by F-16s of the 614th TFS/401st TFW on Ali Al Salem and Al-Jaber airfields.

'We had target priorities based on SAM types, with "Coors 35" prioritised for SA-2, SA-6 and SA-3 and "Coors 36" for SA-3, SA-2 and SA-6 in that order. Normally, we targeted the area first and then the type of SAM. Since we were now only two F-4Gs going into the target area, "Coors 35" and "36" would focus on covering the full area to the best of our ability, concentrating on direct support for the attack missions.

'We stepped to the aircraft and started, taxiing on time. After take-off, we joined on the tanker "Walleye 62" and took a full load of fuel. It was during the turn on the tanker that we realised how strong the winds were as we started banking at the right place but rolled out about 20 miles south of where we wanted to be. As we turned to the north, I caught sight of

All fully armed with four AGM-88s apiece, F-4Gs from Shaikh Isa climb over the Bahraini coastline in close formation during *Desert Storm*. The two jets closest to the camera are from the 561st TFS, while the remaining pair of F-4Gs are 81st TFS machines (*USAF*)

the F-16s from the 614th TFS flight. We were supposed to be in front of them, and instead they were about ten miles in front of us. We could see another F-16 flight on radar, further ahead.

'Our flight plan called for us to take on more fuel as we flew north to the drop-off point, but as we were further south than we planned, we decided to depart the tanker and push it up as fast as possible to the target area. So, we climbed away from the tanker and contacted the AWACS (I think its callsign was "Ponca"). This was about the time that the F-16 pilots were asking about the status of the *Weasels*. I made a call to them that we were only a flight of two, and were several miles behind them. I recommended that they made a 360-degree turn so that we could close the gap, but they answered negatively and continued on to their targets.

'We were at about 28,000 ft and 0.95 Mach. "Coors 35" was on the left and I was to his right in line abreast formation. I could see the 614th FS F-16s to my right at about ten miles, but our route had us diverging slightly. I tried to split the difference between following my leader, "Coors 35", and supporting the attack force, so I angled right to keep them in sight. About this time the F-16s stirred up the SAMs to the north and west. We had several SAMs displayed on our nose, with good ranging on our AN/APR-47. We selected the closest SA-6 to their target area and fired a HARM. This was a long-range shot (about 40 miles, with flight time of two-and-a-half minutes). We immediately followed this with another shot at an SA-6 in the same vicinity. The second shot was at about 35 miles, with about a two-minute time of flight.

'In firing the first two missiles, I lost sight of my element lead and continued veering to the right. Next, we fired at an SA-2 to the east in the vicinity of the 614th TFS target area from about 15 miles. The first three shots took place in about a minute. After the third shot I rolled out on a northerly heading and tried to find both my flight leader and the 614th TFS jets.

'A few seconds later we had a "pop-up" [range unknown] launching SAM in the 614th TFS target area. It was at about ten miles and about

20 degrees to the right of our nose. It came up initially as an SA-6 but I
believe it was ambiguous, and it resolved to an SA-2 later. I turned to put
the SAM on the nose to reduce missile time of flight, and Don Whittler
did the hand-off. As soon as we rolled out, we took the shot. As the
missile came off, it made the right engine's compressor stall, but it went
like a spear directly towards the SAM's location. I followed the missile's
flight for a short time, but then lost it in the clouds and background.
I recovered the F-4G's right engine and turned back to the north. As
I rolled out, I saw some vertical contrails that it finally dawned on me
were made by SAMs. I also saw several black smudges that were either
SAM or AAA explosions.

'As I was taking in the view, I checked my gauges to ensure that I still had
plenty of fuel remaining. However, I was now out of missiles. I could hear
that the F-16 flights were departing their target areas. I finally realised that
I was alone, heading north, and decided it was not a good idea to continue
on this flightpath, so I did a 180 and headed south. I calculated that we had
more than enough fuel to make it back to Shaikh Isa, so we bypassed our
post-strike refuelling. I didn't see my flight leader again until we arrived back
on the ground. We did a quick Intelligence and Maintenance debriefing and
then reviewed our tapes.

'A few days later I talked to "Orville" Wright about the mission. He pointed
out that Capt Phil M Ruhlman [Standards and Evaluation Officer of the
401st TFW – he later became a Brigadier General] owed me a case of whisky
for saving his life. All I knew was that we fired a missile at a launching SAM
and most likely took it out. "Orville" told me the rest of the story. Phil was
in a serious defensive manoeuvre [in his F-16C] when our HARM came in
and took out the SAM radar.

'As for an analysis of the timing while supporting the 614th TFS mission,
had we been on time and ahead of the task force we would not have been in
a position to make as rapid a shot as we made. If we had been past the target
area, rather than pointing at it, there would have been a longer turn to get
the target onto our nose, which would have resulted in a longer missile time
of flight. On future missions we made it a point to keep the nose onto the
target area whenever possible.

'After about two days the SAM density in the KTO was reduced significantly,
and the Wing needed the flexibility to fly all aircraft throughout the theatre,
so the F-4G squadron uploaded wing fuel tanks again and went back to the
"two HARM, three fuel tank" configuration. Having been lucky enough to
fly a four HARM, single tank F-4G into a target-rich environment was the
highlight of my career!'

Compressor stalls caught one of Lt Col Gelwix's 'Pearl' flight crews
unawares on the first night too, as Col Uken recalled;

'Our No 3 aircraft, about four minutes after crossing the border, radioed
"'Pearl 3' is wounded bird [battle damage], egressing south". A minute
later came "'Pearl 3' is back in", followed by third and fourth radio calls of
"'Three' is wounded bird' and "'Three' is back in'. I told Lt Col Gelwix,
"Boy, 'Pearl 3' is really taking a pounding! I hope they can make it over
the border".

'It turned out that every time he fired a HARM he was giving himself
an engine compressor stall, which, with a J79 engine, could produce quite

The pilot's right-hand side panels accommodated (from the left) the master caution lights, radio controls, IFF controls, the bomb control panel and compass controls. The combined oxygen hose and communications leads are at the bottom of the photograph (*Author's Collection*)

a bang and a bucking motion. In the fog and friction of war he had forgotten basic rule No 1 – when firing a HARM, turn away from the shot, as the rocket engine exhaust is likely to give you a compressor stall. He was hearing a bang, feeling the F-4 shake and watching an engine wind down on its own. In each case, after turning south he was able to re-start the engine, and since all appeared normal, return to the fight. It wasn't until his fourth shot that he remembered to turn away from the side that the HARM was being launched from.'

Lt Col Gelwix and Maj Uken were amazed by the amount of AAA that rose towards them as they penetrated seven miles across the border. Numerous IRG SA-6s were active, and Uken had 'the top 15' showing on his scope. 'After our first SAM break, our RWR scope quickly displayed multiple SA-2, SA-3 and SA-6 sites in various modes of operation from searching, to tracking, to launching at someone else, to launching on you. Every HARM I shot was against an SA-6 either shooting at us or someone not too far from us. As they say, a target-rich environment. If we'd had more gas and HARMs we could easily have shot a dozen or more'.

His crew were credited with three successful shots against SA-6s on the night of 17 January, with two definite SA-6 kills and a 'probable'. The Baghdad crews had similar experiences, with the occasional IrAF MiG or Mirage F1EQ to handle as well. *Weasel* crews had been told to expect 20 to 30 per cent losses against these formidable defences, but on the first night they all returned intact. One HARM may have gone astray. A B-52G (later nicknamed 'In HARM's Way') was reportedly damaged by an AGM-88 that homed onto the fire-control radar of its tail guns after an F-4G was mistaken for an IrAF MiG by the bomber's gunner. From 1 October 1991, all B-52G tail guns were removed.

Lt Col Walton led 52nd TFW F-4Gs against targets 'around the perimeter of Baghdad', where they encountered 'lots of AAA' but only one SAM. As he pointed out, the combination of the AN/APR-47 and HARM meant that they could distance themselves from the threat. However, on other missions, unexpected SAMs were sometimes launched from immediately under the *Weasels*, requiring traditional SAM evasion manoeuvres.

HARM was effective at both very long ranges and from close quarters. For Col Redmond, 'My shortest shot was at a range of just 3.5 miles against an SA-6 battery that had proved to be difficult to kill in Kuwait, so "John Boy" [Lt Col George Walton] and I went out with the express purpose of ramming a HARM down its throat. The Block 3 HARM had a speed of almost Mach 4, and we believed that we could get the missile's time of flight down to eight to ten seconds if we shot at that close range.

'We went in as a single ship, with our wingman outside the threat ring and looking for other threats (Scott Gounad and 'Buster' Crabbe were our No 2, and they did a great job). We got ELINT on the SA-6 and took the shot at 3.5 miles. We then immediately broke away, using all the chaff we carried in a preventative mode. "John Boy", who had the eyes of an eagle – better than my 20–10 vision – saw the HARM hit and the SA-6 radar never came up again.'

On Night One, Gelwix and Uken, in F-4G 69-0232 'Pearl 51', were the first crew to return to Shaikh Isa, having watched 'the arcs and some detonations of Scud missiles along the Saudi coastal region'. As they arrived and reached the end of the runway for post-flight checks, Maj Uken saw 'a sight I will never forget. The entire 10,000 ft parallel taxi way was lined with Marines and airmen as we made our way back to the south end and our parking area. All were either saluting or jumping up and down with excitement, as they knew that beating the Iraqis was our quickest way home after five months there.

'After engine shutdown, and a quick word with some very relieved crew chiefs, it was over to Intel for a verbal debrief and to hand them our CONRAC recorder – it copied everything that the RWR had "seen", the HARM shots taken, emitter parametric data, etc. They wanted us to try and get some rest as our next mission was in eight hours.'

One of the most hazardous early attacks was made by F-117As and F-111Fs on the chemical and biological production site at Salman Pak, with F-4G support led by Maj Bart Quinn with Capt Ken Hanson – a team who would eventually score six SAM site kills. They had been warned that captured Kuwaiti I-HAWK SAMs might be used, with some chance of success, against the F-117As. There were also SA-8s and SA-3s in the area posing severe threats to the 48th TFW F-111Fs as they made their low-altitude laser-guided bomb attacks on the bunkers storing anthrax. An SA-8 battery was destroyed by a HARM from Quinn's jet.

Although an F-15E and an F/A-18A were lost to air-defence missiles during the first night of *Desert Storm*, more than 1000 Coalition aircraft had hit their targets thanks to the outstanding success enjoyed by the *Weasels*. Some 56 SAM and AAA radar installations had been destroyed by the 125 HARMs that they fired, crippling the Iraqi IADS in the Kuwait sector and causing major damage to defences within Iraq too.

The main problem, as noted by Lt Gen Glosson, was that the USAF 'did not have enough F-4Gs to find all the radar sites in Iraq. But I wanted the Iraqis to think that we did'. The solution, suggested by chief IADS planner Brig Gen Larry 'Poobah' Henry, was to use the US Navy's F/A-18 Hornets as additional HARM launchers. In the resulting 'Poobah's Party', drones went in first to flush out the enemy radar systems. A barrage of HARMs would then descend upon them from up to 60 shooters, forcing operators to turn off their surviving radars and fire missiles and AAA ballistically.

The F-4Gs could attack specific sites using their AN/APR-47s. The Hornets, lacking similar equipment, just fired pre-emptive barrages of HARMs into areas that were known to have IADS radar installations so that they could home onto any that came up. It was a devastating, decisive blow, both in terms of IADS assets destroyed and as a psychological assault on Iraq's supposedly impregnable defences.

CHAPTER FIVE

STORMING AHEAD

Maintainers and refuellers work on a line of 561st TFS/35th TFW(P) F-4Gs at Shaikh Isa AB prior to the aircraft receiving ordnance for the night's missions over Kuwait and Iraq. Aircrew flying in *Desert Storm* normally removed squadron patches from their flightsuits, displaying only a small name tag with a callsign (*Terry Panopalis Collection*)

easel operations continued in the unusually bad weather following the second night of *Desert Storm*. Despite thick fog, the Shaikh Isa aircraft were required to protect air strikes, including the ongoing B-52 night assaults on the IRG in Kuwait. After three days of fighting, the *Weasel* missions were divided between Direct Support of specific strike packages and Area Suppression, for which a group of F-4Gs would support a series of strikes over a wide area, tackling targets of opportunity that threatened any of the strike packages. Crews involved in the latter missions were christened the '*Weasel* Police'.

By 26 January, the desire for protection by *Weasels* had become a prerequisite for organisers of all strike packages, but there was a shortage of such aircraft. The remedy, devised by Lt Col Ballanco and Maj Uken, was to mount a combat air patrol (CAP) of *Weasels* that would be available for a set time to cover scheduled targets. As Uken explained, 'After ten to 14 days, we could take a two-ship of F-4Gs and cover all of Kuwait and a large portion of southeast Iraq to a radius of 100 miles, and any threats that popped up we would attempt to neutralise with HARMs. We would aim to spend a half-hour on station. Any number of strikes would be going on – B-52s, A-10As, F-16s, AV-8Bs etc. Our role was to support their different times on target.

'In reality there were so many different attacks going on at the same time that quite often we would not be capable of being in a position to support two packages at the same time. If a threat popped up in proximity to someone that we could not support, we could at least provide a radio call to warn them of the nature of the threat.'

The essential role of the *Weasels* was underlined on the second night of the campaign when 48 F-16s in two packages were sent to bomb Baghdad's nuclear research facility. Due to a series of misunderstandings, the F-4Gs were late and there were delays for inflight refuelling so that only one F-16 package had SEAD and air-to-air support over a heavily defended site. Two F-16s were lost to SAMs from the package that lacked *Weasel* protection.

Lt Gen Glosson reinforced the need for SEAD on all such missions in future. He made it clear to his commanders, including the SAC B-52 managers, that they should not revert to flying at the low altitudes for which they had been trained just because the main SAM threat was being reduced after the first two nights. He was well aware that the vast numbers of AAA, MANPADS and other short-range SAMs, particularly around Baghdad and Mosul, still made flying at less than medium altitude far too risky.

A *Weasel* four-ship would offer three hours of availability by cycling one pair onto a tanker while the other pair maintained the CAP. They could then cover a succession of pre-planned strikes in a target box identified by map grid lines. This 'Weasel Police' (or 'Weasels on Patrol') tactic worked particularly well in Kuwait, offering 24-hour coverage, but over Iraq the area requiring coverage was far greater, and *Weasels* were generally allocated to Direct Support for specific long-range strikes. By that time the SAM threat had been much reduced, and some *Weasel* crews were flying several missions without getting an opportunity to fire HARMs.

Meanwhile, flights of four or six F-4Gs were providing Direct Support for formations of up to 60 F-16s attacking military objectives in the Baghdad area. Generally, as Col Uken described, 'On *Desert Storm* missions we tried to get in five minutes before the strike package and stay on station throughout the ToT [Time on Target] of the strike. That time depended on the number of strike packages sequenced through the target. In a lot of cases, the *Weasels* were the last ones out. Of importance to us was the strike package's ability to compress the ToT, reducing the time on station for the *Weasels*.'

Flying *Weasels*

The F-4G was essentially an early 1960s jet, only a couple of years younger than its partner in SEAD, the (E)F-111A, and it was a less user-friendly fighter to handle than its F-16 successor in the *Weasel* role. Both crew members sat low in their cockpits, with limited external view, particularly from the rear seat, where vision ahead was virtually non-existent. Forward vision for the pilot on landing was obscured by the long nose and heavy windshield framing, forcing pilots to adjust their seats to have some sort of view ahead.

A lack of forward vision was a particular problem during aerial refuelling, when it was difficult to see the director lights on the tanker's belly that showed the Phantom II pilot his position relative to the Flying Boom refuelling apparatus. The front ejector seat then had to be raised or lowered

so that the pilot could see the lights, rather than his own canopy bow, as he tried to hold his position behind the tanker at around 360 mph.

Although the introduction of leading-edge wing slats on the F-4E had significantly reduced its turning circle in combat, the Phantom II was still decidedly lacking in manoeuvrability when compared with the much younger and more agile F-16, where computers handled much of the workload. F-16s also offered a longer loiter time than the F-4G and, as Col Uken noted, in hunter-killer paired missions 'the F-4G would run out of gas first'. Nevertheless, most Phantom II crews were ardent supporters of their steeds.

The two-HARM, two-Maverick configuration gave the F-4G a far more effective stand-off SEAD/DEAD capability than conventionally armed fighter-bombers that relied on short-range missiles and unguided iron bombs. Maverick, with a range of more than 14 miles, was a crucial weapon in the relief of Kuwait. More than 5000 were fired by US tactical aircraft, with those expended by the USAF achieving a 90 per cent hit rate. The infra-red imaging AGM-65D was the most widely used, and it achieved success against targets such as mobile missile launchers, homing in on hot metal surfaces that had absorbed the sun's heat (*USAF*)

Wing slats could also cause sudden changes in pitch when they abruptly extended automatically during in-flight refuelling as the Phantom II's angle of attack increased with the weight of additional fuel. They were useful in increasing the aircraft's rate of turn when the crew had to make a steep diving turn in afterburner as part of a standard SAM avoidance manoeuvre, accompanied by chaff and jamming from the F-4G's ECM pod. Range considerations in Iraq meant that afterburner had to be used sparingly, for it increased fuel consumption by more than 300 per cent. With a full load of four HARMs and a single centreline tank, an F-4G could still cruise at almost 630 mph.

Take-off was normally at around 215 mph, having advanced the throttles to 85 per cent before releasing the brakes and lighting afterburners. For combat missions with live ordnance, separation of 20 seconds from the preceding aircraft was required at take-off. Maximum weight on take-off was 62,000 lbs. Landing gear and flaps were raised at 230 mph, well before the gear and flap limit speed of 290 mph.

Afterburners, gobbling fuel at up to 90,000 lbs per hour, were disengaged at around 400 mph, having consumed up to ten per cent of the onboard fuel. In normal climb speed (at just below full non-afterburning 'military' power), fuel consumption was a more tolerable 14,000 lbs per hour by both J79-GE-17 engines. Nevertheless, a combat flight of F-4Gs had to seek a tanker within around 25 minutes of take-off in order to have enough fuel to accomplish the main element of the mission during *Desert Storm*.

Aerial refuelling was part of each day's work. The tankers flew along set tracks, around three miles apart, in trail formation at set altitudes that provided a 'High' tanker, a 'Medium' height example and one at the front of the trio in the 'Low' position. The tanker tracks were initially placed around 100 miles south of the Iraqi border, reducing the ToT for many aircraft, particularly if they encountered emergencies or had to face MiGs. Tanker crews would also routinely move closer to the border to rescue

fuel-starved fighters. In order to save time during the first stages of the campaign, F-4Gs were often 'hot pitted' after missions by refuelling them and changing the crew on the ground while the engines were left idling. A turnaround in about five minutes was then possible.

Fuel starvation was the main cause of the only F-4G loss during the war. The crew involved, Capt Tim Burke and EWO Capt Juan Galindez of the 81st TFS, were protecting a 19–20 January F-111F night strike package as part of a four-ship 'Falstaff' flight led by Capt Vinnie Quinn and Maj Ken Spaar against the massive Al Taqqadum air base, part of the H2 and H3 airfield complex in western Iraq. Although they encountered no hostile radars, and kept their HARMs, the flight met very bad weather as it left the target in search of a post-strike tanker.

Because their mission crossed the midnight deadline between sections of the ATO, all the callsigns and radio frequencies for the tankers changed at that moment, as did 'squawks' in the aircrafts' identification friend or foe (IFF) transponder signatures. The *Weasels*, whose take-off had been delayed, did not receive the updates and were therefore unable to communicate with other flights, including the tankers – they were also at risk of interception by Coalition fighters.

Capt Quinn picked up on radar what looked like a tanker flight and moved towards it in thick cloud, only to find himself behind a B-52G bomber cell, flying in trail and presumably refuelling. He flew to the front of the procession as his fuel neared the red line, found the tanker and used the secure Guard frequency to persuade the tanker captain to interrupt his B-52 fill-up session and plug into the *Weasel* instead.

Burke and Galindez, as 'Falstaff 03', sought their own tanker via the AWACS controller, but a navigation error placed their F-4G 60 miles off the expected refuelling meet-up point. Burke turned towards the new heading, only for the Phantom II and the tanker to miss each other in the appalling weather. Now low on fuel, he had to forego the chance of trying to catch the tanker.

After two hours attempting to locate and link up with a tanker, Burke finally headed for the diversion airfield at King Khalid Military City in Saudi Arabia. As he descended, he found that the fog at an altitude of 400 ft was thick right down to ground level. Lacking adequate runway lighting for the weather conditions, Burke made three missed landing approaches and was down to 400 lbs of fuel as he attempted a fourth.

The 81st TFS's F-4G-42-MC 69-0250 had a vari-ramp filled with 12 radar site kill markings, making it the top scorer for the squadron during *Desert Storm*. Even that achievement was not enough for it to escape the QF-4G conversion line (in 1998) following seven years in storage at AMARC (*T Panopalis Collection*)

Pulling away once again, the fuel was close to exhaustion and both crew ejected, Galindez landing on the runway and Burke to the left of it. F-4G 69-7571 flew on for a mile and landed itself in the sand, remarkably undamaged but beyond recovery.

Examination of the airframe showed that one of the external wing tanks had a few bullet holes in it, so the loss was somewhat controversially attributed to fuel leakage due to combat damage. Burke and Galindez were flying again two days later.

En route to a *Weasel* target area, chaff systems were armed and tested and radar, ordnance and radar warning systems checked as a pair of F-4Gs cruised 500 ft apart at around 0.83 Mach. The ideal cruising altitude was around 20,000–25,000ft where the aircraft's stability, manoeuvrability and fuel consumption were at their most favourable.

At the beginning of the war, few Coalition pilots had seen the white smoke trail of a HARM launch, and *Weasel* pilots hardly ever made live firings during peacetime sorties. On several occasions, strike or fighter formations thought they were under attack by air-to-air missiles from IrAF fighters, which still presented a threat, or a SAM. F-4G pilots quickly adopted a reassuring standard call of 'Magnum!' for that situation, as Col Uken explained;

'We started calling "Magnum" to show that we were responsible for the missile in the air. "Magnum" goes back to Vietnam when a Shrike launch got a "Shotgun" call – which was still in use in 1991. When we started firing Mavericks from F-4Gs we used a "Rifle" call, so a natural evolution was "Magnum" for the HARM'. In some cases aircraft that were flying a single-ship reconnaissance mission, or in a strike package unsupported by *Weasels*, would use "beer" callsigns hoping to decoy the enemy into thinking that *Weasels* were in the vicinity, even to the extent of making the occasional "Magnum" call. The *Weasels* themselves would sometimes continue to make "Magnum" calls after they had used up all their HARMs in order to deter the missile batteries from attempting to engage strike aircraft.'

The 'beer' callsigns ('Nicolaub', 'Schlitz', 'Lone Star', 'Coors', 'Bud', etc.) were allocated to *Weasel* flights randomly for each day's 'frag' (fragment of the operational schedule for the day's missions) order, and they soon became familiar trademarks for the F-4Gs as Uken noted;

'When strike flights checked in with AWACS, they would ask if there were any beer callsigns airborne. We would respond, and they would ask what the ground situation was like. The F-15Cs used gas station callsigns, F-16s used dog breeds, the tankers were fish or oil companies, F-15Es were cars ("Chevy", etc.), F-111E/Fs were US football teams, EF-111As were tools like "Wrench", "Pliers", etc. The RF-4Cs were trees and the A-10As used gun names like "Colt" and "Luger".'

When *Weasels* were cleared to fire at a target, the call was 'Buntari'. Callsigns could be borrowed from other aircraft types for a day to confuse the Iraqis. F-15C and F-4G pilots sometimes adopted the tankers' oil brand callsigns to catch IrAF fighter pilots off guard, and Eagles briefly sported beer callsigns to reduce the ground-to-air opposition.

F-4G crews took advantage of the HARM's long range in attacks on the heavily defended Baghdad area, as Col William Redmond recalled;

'My longest-range shot was at 52 miles on an SA-8 acquisition radar that seemed to be the main such system in southeast Baghdad. We had destroyed the SAMs in the eastern part of Baghdad pretty well on the first night [of *Desert Storm*] during my mission with "John Boy" [Walton] in "Lonestar" flight on the night of 17–18 January, and also during an 81st TFS mission by Maj Bart Quinn and Capt Ken Hanson ["Hamms 61" against an Al Jarrah target]. Two weeks later, I believe, they moved some SA-6s and SA-8s in to fill the gaps in the air defence.

'We had terrible weather, late tankers and were a minute late for our protection role for about 26 F-111s. It was our job to put ourselves between the threat and the attacking F-111s. I was working the electronic order of battle and noticed that the flight time for a HARM would put us four seconds early for the ToT if I fired at 52 miles out. I started laughing because we would then make our ToT.

F-4G-43-MC 69-7212 scored five radar kills (proudly presented here in an unusually large format) in 60 missions during *Desert Storm*. It served as the CO's aircraft for the 52nd TFW at Shaikh Isa AB during the campaign (*Author's Collection*)

'I crew-coordinated with "John Boy" and let it [HARM] rip, and after about four minutes we went into a pretty good hornet's nest, with the SAMs on the east side. I checked during the missile's time of flight and the SA-8 went off the air. My post-analysis for the next five days showed that it never came up again, so I logged it as a probable kill. We expended all of our HARMs (we were a four-ship flight) in about a minute-and-a-half when we got within about 12 miles of the target and they started firing SA-6s at us, but our jamming and manoeuvres defeated them.

'After it got quiet, the Mission Commander of the F-111s called and said he was taking a 12-ship to the back-up target because of weather obscuring the primary target. "John Boy" told him we could support him, but we were out of missiles. He asked what happened, and "John Boy" replied "We were in a helluva fight here". I believe they bought us a case of scotch when they learned about it post-mission.'

Weasel support also extended to the B-52 strikes on the IRG divisions whose tanks and artillery were embedded in the Kuwaiti desert. Flying at 30,000 ft, the ponderous bombers were as vulnerable to SA-2s as they had been in Vietnam, but other more potent SAMs were also awaiting them in 1991. The designated F-4G flights flew ahead of the bomber cells, making pre-emptive HARM launches at the threat sites that had the improved SA-2D/E missiles.

Maj Steve Jenny and Capt Mark Buccigrossi were each awarded the Silver Star for a mission on 18 January in which they diverted three pairs of SA-2s away from a cell of B-52s. Using chaff, their ECM pod and

SAM evasion manoeuvres, they caused the missiles to explode harmlessly behind their F-4G.

There was almost a B-52 shoot-down on 28 January when four SA-3s and an SA-2 were launched from Al-Qaim, a site which had already been so heavily bombed that it was considered to be free of missile batteries. The B-52s had been diverted to that target unbeknown to the SEAD force, so no *Weasels* were on hand. This led to Lt Gen Glosson's policy of destroying all SAM sites until there was 'nothing but sand out there' through an increased SEAD effort. He told Maj Gen Glenn Profitt, Director of Electronic Combat for *Desert Storm*, that he wanted a chart to show him every SAM site, and the date on which it had been destroyed.

Maj Uken and Lt Col Gelwix scored their 'most satisfying HARM shot ever' on Night 4 (20 January 1991) during a support mission for 'Boston 30', a cell of B-52s hitting the Medina Republican Guard Division headquarters in Kuwait. As the F-4G crew prepared to take off in 'Michelob 61' (F-4G 69-0270, which ended *Desert Storm* credited with five radar kills), they were told that their tanker aircraft had aborted and there were no spares. Uken explained what then transpired;

'Knowing that the B-52s had already departed Cairo West airfield [in Egypt] and were flying across the barren lands of western Iraq, we were betting that they were unaware of our dilemma. With only a centreline tank, and four HARMs, we knew we were already going to be well beyond our minimum fuel plan, including a pre-strike refuelling. Despite having no chance of a post-attack refuelling, we were committed to the support task anyway, even if it meant having to land short at one of the Coalition bases just south of the Kuwaiti border.

'Loss of the tanker required some re-planning. We told the rest of "Michelob" F-4G flight to stand by while we came up with a plan. After plugging the target coordinates into the INS, arriving at a straight-line distance and calculating flight time and fuel requirements, it became apparent that we could get to the target, but would have no loiter time. To cover the B-52s' vulnerability period in the threat ring, we decided on breaking the flight into four single aircraft with 20-mile spacing in trail formation to extend our collective on-station time. After calculating take-off time, we called the other jets in "Michelob" flight and explained the amended plan to them.

'Once airborne it all went pretty much as planned, and as we approached the target from the south we were able to find "Boston 30" on radar still about 15 miles from the threat ring. Less than a minute later, an SA-6 target tracking radar came up and we started working him. As the B-52s were still outside the threat ring, we calculated that the SA-6 was focused on them, so we delayed the shot for a few seconds. We fired, made the perfunctory "Magnum" call and verified the missile's Time to Impact cue, which looked good.

'Just as the SA-6's missile guidance radar came up, we got an excited call from the EWO in the lead B-52 informing us that he thought they were going to shoot. I was able to tell him "Okay, HARM time to impact is x seconds". The HARM fly-out cue soon showed ":00", and four seconds later the SA-6 "went dotted" [off the air]. "Boston 30" had one happy aircraft commander, who promised us a case of scotch (still waiting for it).

'"Michelob 62" then called "In position" as we turned south for our "skosh" egress and headed for home plate. We "zoomed for the moon" for fuel [economy], did our best imitation of a Space Shuttle descent and were able to make it back to Shaikh Isa after logging a single bag [one drop tank] mission of just 1.9 combat hours.'

Later in the war F-4Gs would join the frantic 'Scud hunt' by Coalition aircraft trying the detect the launch sites for these ground-to-ground tactical ballistic missiles as they were fired towards Saudi Arabia, Bahrain and Israel. This led to some extremely long missions with multiple refuelling requirements, made all the more difficult by the general requirement to switch off all external lighting on the aircraft. Radars and TACAN also had to be turned off when a strike package from the north skirted the potentially hostile Syrian border area. On the night of 21 January, an F-4G crewed by Maj Bart Quinn and Capt Ken Hanson were airborne for 11.25 hours looking for Scuds and SAMs.

WEASELS FROM THE NORTH

By mid-January there were 48 F-4Gs covering Kuwait and the southern areas of Iraq, but the battle area was vast and more were needed to protect forces attacking targets in the northern sections from Incirlik AB in Turkey. The 23rd TFS from Spangdahlem, led by Lt Col David Moody, deployed 12 F-4Gs to Joint Task Force *Proven Force* at Incirlik AB on 16 January as part of the 7440th Composite Wing (CW), which included more than 80 aircraft from several wings. F-111Es, F-16Cs, F-15Cs, F-4Es and RF-4Cs were supported by AWACS aircraft, KC-135As and C-130s. It was a smaller wartime component than the Saudi-based force, but the wing caused considerable overcrowding at the Turkish base, which at least had an Officers' Club with a bar.

Unlike the Shaikh Isa *Weasels*, the 23rd TFS had hunter-killer F-16CJs as part of the SEAD team, and they would fly 900 combat sorties together by the time they left Turkey on 15 March 1991. Their speciality was to attack unexpected mobile ground-to-air threats as targets of opportunity. HARM-carrying F-16CJs could also operate in 'range known' mode, hitting SAM sites whose position was plotted through previous reconnaissance. For this, the HARM targeting system had to be precisely programmed before the mission.

For a team effort with an F-4G, the 'range unknown' method could be used. An emitting radar target could be located by the F-4G and

F-4G-42-MC 69-0285 of the 52nd FW's 23rd FS was one of 12 Phantom IIs deployed to Incirlik AB to serve with the 7440th CW. Seen here shortly after returning to Spangdahlem (and still devoid of its squadron crest), the jet has a prodigious scoreboard of 31 missions on its port vari-ramp. The aircraft silhouette denotes a Maverick hit on a parked IrAF Il-76 on 2 February 1991 during a SEAD mission for F-16s from the 7440th (*T Panopalis Collection*)

F-4Gs 69-7561 and 69-0251 of the 37th TFW explore inhospitable terrain. The four-HARM configuration was favoured for shorter-range operations in *Desert Storm*, although most missions required extra fuel tanks in place of the outboard missiles (*T Panopalis Collection*)

the targeting data was then passed to the F-16. Incirlik-based F-4Gs and F-16CJs flying over the northern part of Iraq from 19 January began to demolish the Iraqi early warning radars around the country's main military targets. HARM was the weapon of choice, with Col Dittmer of the 23rd TFS asserting that 'there were no Shrikes fired in *Desert Storm* from the north', although some were used in later operations.

The task for the 23rd TFS was formidable, as Iraq had received an estimated 10,000 interception radars and 13,000 SAMs from the Soviet Union. When a hunter-killer pair entered the target area, the F-4G was around 8000 ft abeam of the F-16CJ, and they might range up to 250 miles into hostile territory. Another pair was a mile away so that the four-ship maintained a 'fluid four' formation, with plenty of room to manoeuvre and avoid threats. This formation also presented a wide-spread target to ground radars. Top cover was provided by F-15Cs, with EF-111As on hand for radar jamming protection. When the strikers reached the target area, the *Weasels* would set up CAP orbits at a suitable distance from known SAM sites.

Incirlik squadrons worked to their own ATO, coordinating with the Southern ATO each day and focusing on the 7440th CW missions to the north of Baghdad. Col Uken recalled that there was 'little or no liaison between the *Weasel* squadrons [at the two bases] with regard to fragging, etc. The Incirlik squadrons were given some autonomy. They flew three waves per day with mass launches [of strike forces], whereas operations from the south were 24 hours per day. They didn't reach Baghdad until Day 30, which was our first interaction with them. We found that we had targets north of Baghdad, while Incirlik was given targets south of Baghdad, which caused us some consternation'.

Later in the war, after the ground offensive began on 24 February, most Incirlik missions were pulled back further north from Baghdad to prevent an inadvertent HARM attack on Coalition air defence units or any other confliction of forces.

For navigation and communications, *Weasel* crews required a reference location on the ground. In the Vietnam War that 'Bullseye' location was usually Hanoi, but in Iraq it could be a city, one of the IrAF's huge airfields or a local geographical feature. *Weasels* also accompanied strike packages of up to 50 F-16Cs, knowing that the bombers would follow their predictable, briefed headings and Initial Points, providing F-4G crews with their last chance to check radars and weapons settings. They would also roll in to attack at pre-determined altitudes. Their ToT had to be accurate to within 30 seconds to ensure correct coordination with other participants in the strike.

Meanwhile, the F-4Gs would be facing some unpredictable missile threats, unexpected mobile SAM launchers and vehicle-mounted AAA, rather than fixed SAM and AAA sites. As well as neutralising as many of those threats as possible, the *Weasel* crews also had to advise the strikers of any missile launches or AAA fire that they saw. Targets were frequently the military facilities around Kirkuk and Mosul, and they were well defended.

Optically guided AAA weapons could be directed at a target more rapidly than radar-guided guns, but they were obviously limited to daylight use, except on some occasions where Iraqi troops had access to night-vision goggles. AAA was a major threat, but it was at least visible to pilots in daylight conditions. At night, when it was much more visible, smaller calibre weapons like the ZSU-23-4 left a tight chain of red 'golf balls' and 57 mm guns fired clips of three shells, sending larger red balls to medium altitude. The heavy 85 mm and 100 mm guns sent single shells to high altitudes with a yellow-white flash. A 100 mm shell could be deadly at high altitude.

On a night mission an F-4G was blown upside down by a near miss from a 100 mm explosion but it had no major damage apart from the loss of one hydraulic system and its AN/ALQ-184 pod. The 561st TFS usually carried this type of pod, rather than the less powerful Westinghouse AN/ALQ-131 issued to the 81st TFS. Pods were only switched on as part of the process of evading SAMs, as they tended to interfere with the AN/APR-47 system if they were used at other times.

CLARK CREWS

The final unit to supply F-4G crews to the desert campaign was the 90th TFS from Clark AFB. Six pilots and WSOs arrived at Shaikh Isa to begin sorties on 1 February, nominally as attrition replacements. However, as no *Weasel* crews had been lost, their role was to relieve the strain on the severely overworked and fatigued personnel in-theatre. The 561st TFS force also received some welcome relief when six crews from the 562nd TFS at George AFB flew in on 27 January to give some of them a day or two's rest.

After the eighth day of conflict, the air-to-air opposition had rapidly diminished following the evacuation of large numbers of IrAF aircraft to Iran, where most would eventually decay in storage. SAM systems in the *Proven Force* areas of interest also began to wind down their efforts, although the prodigious quantities of AAA were still active. *Weasels* began to return to base with HARMs still on their pylons. The emphasis now shifted from SEAD to DEAD in order to eliminate the missile sites and their radar control units.

In a typical twelve- or eight-ship *Weasel* component for a large strike by Incirlik F-111Es or F-16Cs, one flight was ready to deal with any radars that did show themselves in the target area. The other *Weasels* would also have HARMs, combined with AGM-65 Mavericks, while the accompanying F-16Cs were loaded with CBU-87B and CBU-58 CBUs and conventional Mk 82 or Mk 84 'iron bombs' to wreak havoc on any air defence sites. CBUs were particularly effective in detonating unfired SAMs and destroying equipment over a

Armed with two HARMs, a 35th TFW(P) F-4G drops back from a KC-135 after topping off its tanks during a mission from Shaikh Isa AB. Two AGM-88As was a typical loadout for Phantom II *Weasels* during *Desert Shield/Storm* (USAF)

The formidable sight of an F-4G bearing down on its target laden with a pair of AGM-88s, as well as four CBU canisters for a follow-up attack. The Phantom II's characteristic smoke trail, which made it visible from a considerable distance, was reduced by fitting J79-GE-17E/F engines, developing 17,900 lbs of thrust in afterburner. At some throttle settings and altitudes smoke was still evident. Operating below 5000 ft put the Phantoms at particular risk from deadly ZSU-23-4 four-barrelled, quick-firing AAA guided by 'Gun Dish' radar (USAF)

wide area. Any unused ordnance was aimed at targets of opportunity such as parked aircraft, electricity generators and any surviving radars. Attacks on AAA emplacements, which had been the original target for the F-16C bombers, gave way to the goal of destroying as many SAM sites as possible to remove that hazard permanently.

Maverick missiles had been used to a limited extent earlier in the war in the Kuwait area, as Col Kurt Dittmer recalled;

'We carried Mavericks and Shrikes for about two days on some F-4Gs with missions in the KTO. At this point there was little radar activity in the KTO. I went out with that load [Maverick and Shrike] one night and did not have any suitable targets. Also, there was a cloud deck below us that limited where we could use the Maverick.

'The F-4Gs in *Proven Force* had less SAMs to shoot at, and no aircraft at Incirlik, or the B-52s based at Fairford [in Gloucestershire], had any precision weapon capability. The AGM-65 provided that capability, so we in the "Frag Shop" (I was doing the Electronic Combat planning and the target selections) discussed this with the Air Force component of the Joint Task Force leadership and the 23rd TFS. Jets from the latter unit carried mixed loads, as the HARM was the priority weapon. We loaded F-16s with CBUs to bomb AAA and SAM sites, since that became the primary threat to the bomb droppers, although at night they had HARMs only. The F-16s wanted to shoot AGM-65s as well, but no one had trained to do that at Spangdahlem, so we squashed that'.

The 19 February ATO included the first attack on Baghdad by Incirlik-based strikers. For this, the F-4Gs reverted to the four-HARM configuration, while the F-16Cs were loaded with conventional bombs to tackle a huge number of air defence sites. By 26 February, two days before the ceasefire, the Incirlik *Weasels* had completed some 3000 hours of combat time.

During those final days, as Iraqi troops finally headed out of Kuwait and retreated towards Basra after only 100 hours of ground fighting, there were few HARM shots to be had by Shaikh Isa F-4Gs as many potential targets were obscured by bad weather. The unexpectedly poor conditions and heavy cloud cover had proven advantageous to the Iraqis since Night 2, as they interfered with the laser targeting systems used by most of the Coalition's strike aircraft.

CHAPTER SIX

SOUTHERN WATCH

For the Coalition squadrons in-theatre, most flying came to a halt on 28 February 1991 when the Iraqis surrendered. Those who had been deployed the longest – the Langley AFB F-15C and George AFB F-4G units – were quickly scheduled to return home. As Col Jim Uken recalled;

'A handful of each aircraft were kept on alert status just in case. The 561st TFS *Weasels* were able to get all 24 aircraft out on 23 March, with stops at Zaragoza AB and Terre Haute, Indiana. Spangdahlem's 23rd TFS F-4G/F-16 mix left within 48 hours of hostilities ending, using embedded USAFE tanker support to return home. Col Gene Patton, 35th TFW(P) commander, stayed with a handful of wing staff to complete the departure of Shaikh Isa's aircraft. The first half of the 81st TFS redeployed to Spangdahlem on 5 April 1991.

'Post-*Desert Storm* operations were soon labelled Operation *Desert Calm*. CENTCOM wanted to maintain a presence in Iraqi airspace, and to that end 12 F-4Gs and 32 aircrew remained. Typically, they flew at least eight daily sorties, varying take-off times day-to-day in order to maintain an element of unpredictability.'

CENTCOM Forward Command at Riyadh wanted post-*Desert Storm* air operations to be focused primarily in Saudi Arabia and, to a lesser extent, at Al Dhafra AB, in the United Arab Emirates, and Doha. Saudi Arabia agreed to host a *Desert Shield* Coalition force (the 440th Composite

F-4G-43-MC 69-7235 of the 561st TFS/57th Wing (seen here in 1995) carried a MiG kill marking its port vari-ramp for much of its time as an F-4G. Delivered to the USAF as an F-4E in 1970, the aircraft had been used by Capts Fred Sheffler and Mark Massen of the 336th TFS/8th TFW to down a North Vietnamese MiG-21 on 15 August 1972. Flying the Phantom II as part of an eight-aircraft chaff dropping formation, Sheffler had fired an AIM-7E-2 missile at the MiG after it bounced the USAF fighters and overshot the F-4s. At the end of its life, as Fred Sheffler was told, 'Your jet died a glorious death on 5 May 1998 over the Gulf Range' when it 'took an AIM-120 AMRAAM in the face from an F-16' (*Author's Collection*)

Back from *Desert Storm*, where it destroyed five radar sites, F-4G-45-MC 69-7587 of the 81st TFS/52nd TFW makes a smart take-off from Spangdahlem in September 1991 with a post-war complement of AIM-9 Sidewinders as a reminder of the Phantom II's air-to-air capability (*Author's Collection*)

Wing, equipped with F-4Gs, F-15s, F-16s and EF-111As) at Dhahran AB, which became home for many *Wild Weasel* detachments until January 1996. The 12 F-4Gs left at Shaikh Isa duly flew to Dhahran, with the 35th TFW(P) closing down and all transportable buildings and support equipment being trucked across a 50-mile causeway that connected Bahrain with Saudi Arabia.

Maj Bart Quinn, the senior ranking remaining F-4G officer in-theatre, became the detachment commander in charge of 31 other *Weasel* aircrew, almost all of whom had survived the primitive conditions at Shaikh Isa since 26 December 1990 in the first crew rotation. According to Col Uken;

'They were given an entire six-storey building in an almost empty city built by the Saudi government to house the Bedouins, who preferred their desert tents to modern amenities. These buildings became home for F-4G personnel from Spangdahlem, Nellis [from June 1993] and the Idaho ANG for the next five years and nine months. With the closure of George AFB, the Idaho ANG's 190th TFS at Boise became the new F-4G "schoolhouse". They were tasked for an annual rotation, starting in late 1993.'

The F-4G units subsequently completed 15 deployments at three-month intervals, during which time crews very occasionally attacked Iraqi threat radars. *Weasels* employed HARMs and CBUs against air-defence batteries at Mosul and Bashiquah on three occasions in March 1991, and further enforcement strikes occurred until July of that year. With the advent of Operation *Provide Comfort* from Incirlik and *Desert Calm* from Dhahran, together with the UN-sanctioned Operations *Southern Watch* (OSW) and *Northern Watch* (ONW) from April 1992, the F-4Gs began another set of rotations that required deployed aircraft at both bases. Two no-fly zones were created over Iraq – one north of the 34th parallel and a second from the 32nd parallel south to the Saudi border.

'It soon became apparent to CENTCOM that our presence in enforcing the no-fly zones wasn't going to end any time soon', Col Uken explained. 'With the drawdown of F-4Gs at George already underway [the 561st FS was the last unit to be deactivated here on 30 June 1992, and its aircraft went to the Idaho ANG or into storage with AMARC at Davis–Monthan AFB, Arizona], the closure of Clark AB and the announcement that all *Weasel* operations would be consolidated in the 81st FS, the USAF was scrambling for a game plan. One of the first measures was cutting the numbers of deployed F-4Gs from 12 to eight and, eventually, six at both Incirlik and Dhahran.

'There was still a conundrum, as the requirement for *Weasel* capability was undeniable, and there was no suitable F-4G replacement. The answer became an F-4G "super squadron" to be located at Nellis AFB. The USAF's logistics types undertook a fleet-wide look and selected around 65 F-4Gs to keep flying with the reactivated 561st FS from 1 February 1993 and the 190th FS of the Idaho ANG [the latter commenced its conversion from the RF-4C in June 1991].

'In the interim, Spangdahlem was left "holding the hot potato". Starting with the 12 F-4Gs that were left behind in-theatre, the 81st and 23rd FSs' F-4G/F-16 mix covered operations at Dhahran and Incirlik, respectively, until the 81st FS absorbed all F-4Gs and crews in January 1992. At Dhahran, the detachment was soon dubbed the "*Weasel* Hostage Crisis", with the same Spangdahlem crews pulling rotations from the Gulf War through to June 1993.

'One enterprising aircrew came up with the idea of a "*Weasel* Hostage Crisis Board" – a 12 ft x 4 ft white plywood board suspended from a balcony, with that title and three hooks to hang numbers signifying days in captivity. It was updated at sunset each evening, and it was a sad day when we had to add a fourth hook. In the end we weren't all that sad about not reaching 2000 days, falling just short at 1980 days of operations over Iraq – our F-4Gs were on the ramp at Shaikh Isa or Dhahran for all but about 45 days.

Boasting four radar kill markings, F-4G-44-MC 69-0286 of the 81st TFS basks in the morning sunshine on the Spangdahlem ramp shortly after its return to Germany from *Desert Shield/Storm*. The 52nd TFW insignia on its port engine intake, removed for its earlier combat tour, had only recently been reapplied when this photograph was taken (*T Panopalis Collection*)

F-4G-42-MC 69-0260 was photographed in front of its hardened aircraft shelter at Spangdahlem in May 1992 adorned with the 'spook' silhouettes that became standardised as mission markings on Incirlik-based 81st TFS Phantom IIs. The first eight aircraft to return from Shaikh Isa to Spangdahlem had confirmed kill markings on them in the form of five-inch vertical HARM silhouettes, apart from 69-7212, which had larger, diagonal HARM markings (*USAF*)

'Many original 81st TFS crews saw seven or eight Southwest Asia rotations between 1990 and 1996. Combined with the "Hostage Crisis" was a "Ground Hog Day" level of sameness. Days and weeks blended together, with only temperature increases and decreases signalling changing seasons and, with the desert heat, easterly winds bringing almost unbearable humidity from the Persian Gulf.'

Despite heavy attrition, Iraq still had fighters and more than 8500 mobile SAMs, as well as countless MANPADs and AAA weapons. Many of the aircraft and IADS were of US or French origin, and being similar to those used by Coalition forces, they caused numerous problems when it came to identification of potential threats. Until late 1992 the greatest threat posed to aircraft patrolling both no-fly zones came from IrAF fighters, resulting in five of the latter being shot down.

The Iraqis were also busy resurrecting their ground-based defences immediately post-*Desert Storm*, as Col Uken recalled;

'Overall, Iraqi surveillance radars were detected, but I am not aware of any SAM or AAA threat radars emitting in no-fly airspace during ONW or OSW. However, intel assets then determined that the Iraqis were systematically installing SA-3 sites in the southern no-fly zone approximately 30 nautical miles apart, east to west, for which a "cease, desist and remove" warning was issued. With proof of the fourth SA-3 site then under construction, an offensive air strike was approved using combined USAF/US Navy assets. As the [F-4G] detachment commander, I became the SEAD package commander for the strike, with six carrier-based EA-6Bs joining us on the ramp at Dhahran for mission planning. On the night of 13 January 1993, a combined strike package was tasked with the simultaneous destruction of all four SA-3 sites.

'Our instructions from Riyadh were quite clear – no HARMs off the rails until first bomb impact. While we observed surveillance radar activity north of the no-fly line on entry, the south was devoid of other radar activity. At first bomb impact it was as if the master circuit breaker for all radars in Iraq had been flipped to "off" as they all ceased emitting immediately. Apparently, they were concerned about being targeted as well.'

Four days later, F-4Gs released missiles at a radar site that had locked onto two French *Armée de l'Air* Jaguars flying a reconnaissance mission.

By December 1993, the 81st TFS (FS from then on) had become an all-F-4G squadron. Lt Col Dan Shelor commanded the unit, followed by Lt Col Uken. F-4G crews would support reconnaissance missions by F-15Es or US Navy aircraft and MiGCAP missions by F-15C Eagles, F-16Cs or French Mirage 2000s. Capt Bruce Benyshek flew many such missions, and described one at the time;

Capt Bruce 'Spike' Benyshek, who, with Capt Larry Allen, took out five radar sites during *Desert Storm* and subsequent Gulf operations. Perched on the 81st TFS commander's F-4G, he is giving the author a guided tour of his workplace (*Author's Collection*)

'We will "push" (leave our first route point) about the same time as the F-15Cs move north to cover us. We will be several minutes in front of the strikers. This allows us to loiter near potential trouble spots, receive radar emissions and build an accurate ground "picture". Our speed is chosen to allow us to remain "in country" for the entire time the strikers would be affected by threats. This window of time is called "vul time" [vulnerability time], and it is spelled out for us in the "frag".

'En route to the push-point, we switch radio frequency to AWACS. Periodically, they will provide us with "picture" calls – a God's eye view of aircraft activity in our area of concern. Leaving the push-point, our wingman automatically moves out to "tactical" – a position abreast of us and 1.5 to three miles out, not at the same altitude as us. In an aerial engagement, if you see one opponent it is very easy to find his wingman if he is level with his leader.

'This spacing adds a degree of complication to "tactical turns" onto a new heading, requiring pilots to routinely practice such manoeuvres so that they can be performed in total radio silence. The leader signals the turn with the visible banking of his jet, causing the wingman to quickly replicate this in a 3g movement in the direction of the turn, followed by the leader at a carefully calculated time.

'The rest of our "vul time" is spent in a similar manner. We will shadow our strikers, perhaps spending a little time in a particular area if we find anything of interest. All the while, AWACS and the "Cappers" will be watching any activity north of the 32nd parallel. Every few minutes

F-4G-43-MC 69-7207 was a veteran of 61 combat missions, and it was credited with the destruction of an Iraqi SA-3 radar on 24 July 1993. Removal of a number of SA-3 sites placed in the no-fly zones in both northern and southern Iraq had commenced 25 days earlier when an F-4G destroyed one on 29 June (*T Panopalis Collection*)

AWACS will provide "picture calls". Of course, we may look with our own radar when we so desire.'

The arrival of the 561st FS at Dhahran, led by Lt Col Dan Constantini, in November 1993 allowed half the remaining Spangdahlem F-4G crews and aircraft to depart for Germany, and thence for follow-on assignments to the 561st. Three months later the remaining 81st FS crews and jets departed Incirlik for Nellis, thus bringing to a close the USAF F-4G operations in Europe.

The enlarged 561st FS had become the biggest fighter squadron in the USAF with 30 F-4Gs, five spares and two maintenance airframes. It also maintained two test F-4Gs at the 422nd Test and Evaluation Squadron. The 561st was now staffed by 600 personnel, with 500 of them tasked with maintaining the unit's veteran Phantom IIs. It performed almost all the southwest Asia deployments before departing ONW in October 1993.

It looked like the end for the F-4G overseas, with the 561st having virtually all of its jets at Nellis for the first time in four years. Lt Col Jim Uken was designated as the next 561st FS CO, and he headed off for a preparatory Air Combat Command course. However, a few days later, 'I received a "get your butt home" message. "Your squadron is preparing to deploy"'. Twenty-four F-4Gs were being prepared so that 18 could fly non-stop to RAF Lakenheath, in Suffolk, for Operation *Vigilant Warrior*. Intelligence sources had calculated that Iraq was about to invade Kuwait again and enter Saudi Arabia.

'We departed Nellis on Wednesday evening and landed at Lakenheath 12.3 hours later. After a day of maintenance, the 18 F-4Gs returned to Dhahran on 15 October 1993. Our maintenance people caught up and immediately prepared each aircraft with two AGM-88s, two AIM-7s and an AN/ALQ-184 ECM pod.

'Groundcrews quickly noticed that a third of the AGM-88s being loaded were failing rail continuity checks. Further investigation revealed that all the failed missiles had been flown on F-16CJs since their arrival. A figure in a small window on top of each missile showed how long the weapon had been activated for, and the numbers we were seeing alarmed us. After talking to the F-16CJ pilots we learned two things. Firstly, as the missile was far more sensitive than the RHAW gear fitted to their jets, they liked using it in the sensor [HAS] mode to augment their HARM Targeting System pods. And secondly, the F-16CJ pilots had no ability in the cockpit to check whether they had a "good" or "bad" missile loaded. Extensive use of the HAS mode was almost certainly creating a software-induced failure of the HARM seeker head.

'It was somewhat deflating to return to "Ground Hog Day"-type activity. It was soon determined that the supposed Iraqi push south was a feint, but it still took the USAF a month to "turn the ship around", with the F-4Gs returning to Nellis on 19 November 1994.'

LAST FLIGHT

By early 1996 the F-4Gs were back at Dhahran again for OSW, although this time their stay was very brief. Indeed, the *Weasels* logged the last combat hours by the Phantom II in US service on 11 January 1996. Having flown the first F-4G into Kuwait on Night 1 of *Desert Storm*, Lt Col Jim Uken was in the same aircraft (69-7232), armed with two HARMs and carrying three fuel tanks, for the last 'O-1' (combat time) mission for USAF F-4s over Iraq. Lt Col Mark Turberville was his pilot in 'Phantom 5' as they patrolled the no-fly zone over southern Iraq. Uken recalled;

'The weather that day was solid undercast, socked in to more than 20,000 ft. The airborne battle commander had already decided to scrub the day's mission, but as we were already on our way in with topped-off tanks, we asked for permission to continue anyway after explaining the significance of this final flight, which was ending an era. It was granted, and 69-7232 was the last US F-4 Phantom II to exit hostile territory. Three days later we left Dhahran, landing at Moron AB, Spain, and Lajes, in the Azores, before a single hop to Nellis from there.'

Returning F-4Gs often made public appearances with their SAM-kill markings painted on the intake vari-ramps, although these were soon removed when they were transferred to other units or to storage. Those markings were of great importance to crews and maintainers who had earned them, as Col Uken explained;

'Every HARM shot taken was tracked by site attacked, location, frequency parametrics, etc. Also tracked were the crew and the jet. When SAM (or other) sites were determined to have been "killed", they were tracked. It was common practice after the Gulf War for deployed jets to be given their "battle markings". The number of kills attributed to each jet was a source of pride for crew chiefs in particular, and a HARM silhouette was painted on the vari-ramp for each. In like fashion, the crew chiefs loved having artwork painted on their jets, and some of it was actually quite good. The jets had to be "tidied up" before being flown home to Nellis, however.'

By the end of *Desert Storm*, the F-4G units involved could legitimately claim that no Coalition aircraft were shot down while *Weasels* were present in their area. Their effort had been a vital component in the Coalition's overwhelming success, although, as with the squadrons flying older types like the F-111 and RF-4C, little publicity was devoted to the *Wild Weasels*. More glamorous new jets like

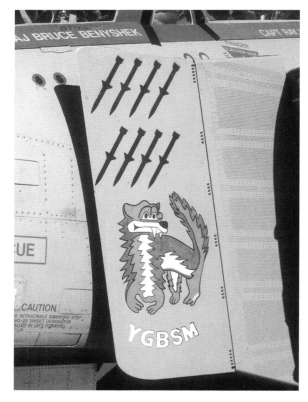

When F-4G-43-MC 69-7232 arrived at AMARC in March 1996 it proudly wore eight radar kill silhouettes, the *Wild Weasel* insignia and *YGBSM* titling on its port vari-ramp. It had been the last USAF Phantom II to exit hostile territory when the jet completed the F-4G's final OSW patrol on 11 January 1996 (*T Panopalis Collection*)

An F-4G rear cockpit, with severely restricted forward visibility, seen in 1995 (*T Panopalis Collection*)

the F-117A and F-15E occupied the headlines and were the subject of USAF Press material.

The small *Weasel* force had worked very hard, and the F-4Gs, despite their age, had attained record in-commission rates that compared well with more recent types. The 81st TFS alone had completed 1167 missions, totalling 4000 combat hours – each mission typically lasted four hours. The three squadrons involved had fired more than 1000 HARMs, and at the end of the conflict the 81st TFS was credited with 142 SAM site kills. The 'high flyer' F-4G (69-7253) in the 81st TFS had completed 62 combat missions, while 69-7207, as the high-time 561st TFS *Weasel*, had flown 61. As Command Historian for SAC, Lt Col Jerome V Martin wrote the following summary of *Weasel* operations in 1994;

'SEAD quickly reduced the threat from radar-guided missiles and forced the Iraqis into ineffectual back-up modes of operation [such as optical guidance]. After Iraqi radar operators virtually halted emissions, the SEAD effort began to attack the undamaged air defence sites that could still threaten Coalition aircraft. The ground forces supported the SEAD campaign with artillery, rocket fire and long-range strikes by the [MGM-140] Army Tactical Missile System (ATACMS) against radar and SAM sites. The SEAD effort was so successful that only ten Coalition aircraft were shot down by SAMs, although the Iraqi defenders fired thousands of the missiles.'

Yet despite being a very credible weapon in 1992, the F-4G was an ageing airframe, and there was no obvious replacement in sight. Updates were still planned to keep it current, but the jet's maintenance costs were becoming prohibitive. Prior to the advent of *Desert Shield/Storm*, the USAF had planned to retire the F-4G in 1990–91 and close George AFB in 1992. The last class of F-4G trainees (Capt David Lucia being the final pilot candidate) was being processed when Kuwait was invaded.

While the installation of the AN/APR-47 system was Phase 1 of the aircraft's PUP, Phase 2 would have included an innovative digital receiver group and a new antenna array. However, as Col Uken put it, the programme 'exceeded the available technology and, after several years, attempts to make it work were shelved'.

Various tactical aircraft were considered as successors to the F-4G in the *Weasel* role including the F-15D/E 'Mud Hen' fitted with the F-4G electronics package, the F-111, Tornado and F-16D. Col Uken was adamant that a two-seat aircraft was necessary, continuing the line of development begun with the F-100F Super Sabre. 'From our point of view, the F-15E Eagle was the only viable candidate', he explained. '"*Weasling*" is a two-seat function, and single-seat is not the way to go'. The choice of the single-seat F-16CJ as the prime SEAD platform was therefore unpopular in many quarters, as veteran crews felt it overloaded the pilot.

Col Kurt Dittmer recalled being in the Pentagon after *Desert Storm* when a lieutenant general 'made an outlandish claim that the F-16 was more survivable than the F-4G. Fellow *Weasels* "Pug" Svestka and Billy Holway joined me to argue this point with the general, as his belief was the precursor to getting the HARM targeting system installed in the F-16 at the expense of the F-4G. We were told that because the F-16 had a better air-to-air radar and manoeuvrability [than the F-4G], it was more survivable. We pointed out that, as a *Weasel*, the F-16 no longer had visibility into the low frequency bands, where finding the early-warning and height-finding radars to cue the SAMs [was necessary], so it would not be as effective or survivable in the SEAD mission. We did not win that argument, but at least we spoke the truth to those in power'.

In late 1991, after its successful deployment by the 23rd FS in *Desert Storm*, proponents of the F-16 welcomed the dedicated F-16CJ *Wild*

In the late 1990s, the F-4G gave way to its former SEAD partner, the smaller F-16CJ – these aircraft from the 81st TFS/52nd TFW were photographed prior to flying a training mission from a damp Spangdahlem. With three tanks and HARM missiles, a combat-loaded F-4G, such as the aircraft seen here, weighed almost 20,000 lbs more on take-off than an F-16CJ (*USAF*)

Weasel variant based on Block 50/52 versions of the General Dynamics fighter. It was seen as a 'Super *Weasel*' that could operate without having to be accompanied by an F-4G in order to provide effective SEAD. The jet's smokeless engine and small dimensions made it less visible, and the use of composite airframe materials reduced its radar signature compared with an F-4G. The F-16CJ's HARM Targeting System was refined in its R7 version to accurately launch precision-guided munitions and destroy SAM sites.

LATTER DAYS

After *Desert Storm*, and the decision to remove the F-4G from active service, 18 aircraft were sent to the Idaho ANG's 190th FS/124th TRG at Boise, Idaho, in the summer of 1991, replacing some of the unit's RF-4Cs. Eventually, 36 F-4Gs were received from the 35th and 52nd TFWs and training was undertaken by the 189th Fighter Flight. In March 1996, shortly after the unit had taken part in a *Red Flag* exercise, the 190th converted again, this time to the C-130 Hercules, and its F-4Gs were retired.

Maintenance costs and the sheer amount of work required to keep the jets airworthy had brought an end to Phantom II operations with the ANG. The fact that groundcrews were finding it increasingly hard to undertake rectification work in inaccessible areas of the airframe (compared with the simple modular fixes for later aircraft like the F-16, in which pull-out black box units could be replaced quickly) made the F-4Gs unviable in an increasingly cost-conscious operating environment. The *Weasel* Phantom II was a highly specialised, one-mission aircraft, and the 'bean counters' thought its job could be done by more versatile

Many Idaho ANG F-4Gs were decorated with a fanged 'weasel mouth' in the style of the 'sharksmouth' marking, which several of them had originally worn when serving as F-4Es with the 388th TFW at Korat RTAFB during the Vietnam War. A few (including 69-0298, 69-7557 and 69-7551) did indeed have F-4E-style 'sharksmouths' applied. F-4G-42-MC 69-0272, seen here in storage at AMARC in October 1997, also had the message *Last flight 4.9.96. Last real Weasel* scribbled on its nose in Sharpie marker pen and stencilling on its port engine intake celebrating the 50,000th F-4G sortie in Operation *Provide Comfort*, flown on 26 September 1995 (*T Panopalis Collection*)

modern types. Many were subsequently expended in the USAF's Aerial Target programme as QF-4Gs, although the 190th FS's 69-7551, which saw combat in Vietnam and *Desert Storm*, was spared and eventually put on display at the Idaho ANG's Gowen Field home.

The Nevada ANG's 192nd TRS/152nd TRG was also scheduled to transition to the F-4G from the RF-4C following *Desert Storm* in 1991. A single aircraft, 69-7580, was delivered to the unit's Reno home and painted in its markings, but the decision was reversed and the squadron remained as an RF-4C reconnaissance unit until 1995, when it too received C-130s.

Post-war a number of conferences were held to discuss the role of the F-4Gs and SEAD, and many of the lessons of the conflict inspired developments in tactics for *Red Flag* and *Green Flag* exercises. Based on the premise that 'you fight like you train', the organisers of the *Flag* programmes felt that their original 'menu' of ten intense sorties per crew, based on Vietnam experience, had been a viable basis for *Weasel* successes in *Desert Storm*.

By 2020, the USAF had been reduced to less than half of its 1991 size, while potential enemies had caught up with many of the innovative weapons that were used so decisively to defeat Iraqi forces, particularly electronic jamming techniques. With the retirement of the F-4G and EF-111A, the escort jamming task passed to the US Navy's EA-6B (and, later, the EA-18G Growler), while SEAD/DEAD continued to be the responsibility of Block 50/52 F-16CJs. These two types now seem to be the last dedicated platforms for the *Wild Weasel* role.

In 2016, as the F-35 Lightning II entered service, it was said to have a 'limited' SEAD capability, but in June 2021 contracts were awarded to modify F-35As from Lot 14/15 production to deliver the AGM-88E/F anti-radiation missile. A new BAe AN/ASQ-239 offensive/defensive EW suite, which would include an anti-radiation missile control system, was also specified. Although the need for dedicated SEAD capability was acknowledged again, in the longer term the *Wild Weasel* task could pass to unmanned platforms.

All but a few F-4Gs ended their days as QF-4G drones. F-4G-43-MC 69-7209, seen here on 21 June 2002, was pulled out of AMARC storage in September 1997 for the Tracor Flight Systems conversion programme into a target drone, after which it was supplied to the 82nd Aerial Targets Squadron of the 53rd Weapons Evaluation Group at Tyndall AFB. The aircraft was expended in a missile test on 1 February 2006 (T Panopalis Collection)

APPENDICES

COLOUR PLATES COMMENTARY

1

F-105F-1-RE 62-4424 *CROWN SEVEN* of the 44th TFS/388th TFW, Korat RTAFB, Thailand, June 1968

Configured as a *Wild Weasel III* and later named *Tyler Rose*, this F-105F was assigned to Majs John Revak and Stan Goldstein, who completed 100 *Wild Weasel* missions during Operation *Rolling Thunder*. It was later modified as an F-105G, with AN/ALQ-105 jammer installations in 'scabbed on' pods along the lower fuselage, and reassigned to the 6010th WWS/388th TFW, with the tail code 'ZB'. Majs William Talley and James Padgett (on his third combat tour) were flying the jet near Hanoi as 'Icebag 01' on 11 May 1972 when, after having evaded six SAMs, they were jumped by a MiG-21 flight and shot down by an 'Atoll' air-to-air missile. Both men became prisoners of war.

2

F-4C-24-MC(ww) 64-0840 *SUPER COCKS SWISS SAMLAR* of the 67th TFS/18th TFW, Korat RTAFB, Thailand, November 1972

An early *Wild Weasel* conversion of the F-4C, 64-0840 initially served with the 66th FWS at Nellis AFB as a trainer for *Weasel* crews, prior to deploying to Korat in late 1972. There, it was assigned to Capts Stu Stegenga and Hans-Peter Zimmermann. They were among the six crews (and maintainers) that participated in Lt Col Don Parkhurst's *Wild Weasel IV* Korat detachment from October 1972 through to February 1973, hence the lettering on the aircraft's intake vari-ramp which stands for 'Don's Dirty Dozen and Crew Chiefs'. The nickname on the nose of the jet includes a reference to the 67th TFS squadron insignia. Reassigned to the Indiana ANG's 113th TFS/181st TFG in 1979, the aircraft was stored at the Aerospace Maintenance and Regeneration Center (AMARC) at Davis-Monthan AFB from October 1987 through to September 1996, when it was sold for scrapping.

3

F-4C-18-MC(ww) 63-7470 *RUB-A-DUB-DUB, TWO MEN IN A TUB* of the 67th TFS/18th TFW, Korat RTAFB, Thailand, December 1972

At Korat, this Phantom II, with formation strip-lights added, was assigned to Majs Robert G Belles and Palmas S Kelly III, who scored a definite radar site kill (VN-266) and a 'probable' (VN-119) in 1972. Seven years later, the aircraft was also assigned to the 113th TFS/181st TFG, where it wore the tail codes 'HF'. 63-7470 eventually became a QF-4C at Tyndall AFB, Florida, for research and testing, and it was lost in an accident flying from there on 19 November 1986.

4

F-4C-23-MC(ww) 64-0757 of the 67th TFS/18th TFW, Kadena AFB, Okinawa, 1972

The 18th TFW briefly sent a detachment of ten F-4C(ww)s – including this jet – to Korat in April 1975 to cover the evacuation of US citizens from Saigon. Aside from flying with the 18th TFW, *Weasel* F-4Cs remained in service at Spangdahlem until July 1979.

Ironically, 64-0757 never served with the 81st TFS in West Germany, but the jet became a fixture at Spangdahlem when it was sent there for bomb-damage repair training after its retirement from the 113th TFS in May 1986. The aircraft was put on display at the Schwabisches Bauern und Technik Museum at Seifertshofen, in Germany, in March 1993, before subsequently moving to the Museo dell'Aviazione di Rimini Ceraboia in Italy in May 1997.

5

F-4G 69-7295-44-MC of the 81st TFS/52nd TFW, Spangdahlem AB, West Germany, 1979

The 52nd TFW's F-4G advanced *Wild Weasels* were initially delivered in their F-4E-style Vietnam camouflage as replacements for F-4Cwws. Ogden Air Logistics Center accepted this aircraft for conversion into an F-4G on 22 March 1979. It subsequently fulfilled the *Weasel* role until the jet was sent for storage at AMARC on 26 March 1996. 69-7295 was eventually converted into a QF-4G drone and expended in August 1999. The AN/ALQ-131(V) ECM pod carried by this jet was generally used by the 81st TFS, and it deployed with AN/ALQ-131(V)-12 pods to Shaikh Isa during *Desert Shield/Storm*.

6

F-4G-44-MC 69-7287 of the 561st TFS/35th TFW, George AFB, California, August 1987

The Euro 1 camouflage scheme with Dark Green FS 34079, Green FS 34102 and Gray FS 36081 was intended to enhance the survivability of tactical aircraft, particularly at low altitudes. This aircraft, which also served with the 563rd TFS/37th TFW at George in Vietnam-era Southeast Asia camouflage, is armed with two AGM-88 HARMs and fitted with a Royal Jet F-15-type 600-gallon centreline tank. 69-7287 was placed in storage at AMARC in June 1992 and revived in 1999 for conversion into a QF-4G aerial target configuration. The aircraft was destroyed in this role in September 2005.

7

F-4G-43-MC 69-7212 of the 23rd TFS/52nd TFW, Spangdahlem AB, West Germany, June 1989

Resplendent in Hill Gray II camouflage (Semi-gloss Gunship Gray FS 26118 and Semi-gloss Medium Gray FS 26270), this *Weasel* would go on to score five SAM site kills in *Desert Storm*. It flew a total of 158 sorties with the 81st TFS from Shaikh Isa AB between 5 September 1990 and 5 April 1991. This was the squadron's third highest mission total, 69-7212 serving as the wing commander's aircraft during the deployment. One of a handful of F-4Gs that initially served with the RAAF as F-4Es in 1970–72, this aircraft was sent to AMARC in December 1995 and sold for scrap 12 years later.

8

F-4G-43-MC 69-7233 of the 561st TFS/35th TFW(P), Shaikh Isa AB, Bahrain, January 1991

This aircraft began conversion from F-4E to F-4G configuration on 30 September 1980 prior to being issued to the 561st TFS at George AFB. It participated in *Desert Shield* from August 1990 and

Desert Storm from January 1991, flying from Shaikh Isa AB. The jet's yellow tail band, unit patches and the TAC insignia on the tail were overpainted for the deployment. 'WW' tail codes were retained throughout the deployment, and these were changed to 'WA' when the squadron was reformed within the 57th Wing for Operations *Provide Comfort* and *Southern Watch*. 561st TFS/FS aircraft usually carried various versions of the AN/ALQ-184(v) ECM pod. 69-7233 was put in storage at AMARC in April 1992 and eventually converted into a QF-4G. It was destroyed as a target in February 2006.

9
F-4G-42-MC 69-0244 *Night Stalker* of the 23rd TFS/7440th CW(P), Incirlik AB, Turkey, February 1991

Nose art was rare on F-4Gs during *Desert Storm*, but some appeared during the later *Provide Comfort* and early OSW periods when squadron markings were also reapplied. Mission markings on Incirlik-based aircraft were applied as miniature versions of the traditional F-4 'Spook' silhouette, carried over to the OSW period when some 23rd TFS aircraft moved to the 81st TFS. *Night Stalker*, however, was among the F-4Gs returned to Spangdahlem and then sent to the USA for storage in February 1992, later to be converted into a QF-4G.

10
F-4G-42-MC 69-0254 of the 561st TFS/4404th CW(P), Dhahran AB, Saudi Arabia, February 1992

Weasels from the 561st FS (with others from the 81st FS) were detached to Dhahran until the 561st was deactivated on 30 June 1992, although this example was already in AMARC storage by May 1992. The aircraft had full wing, squadron and TAC markings reapplied after *Desert Shield/Storm*. The typical loadout during its Dhahran deployment was three drop tanks, two HARMs, two AIM-7F Sparrows and an AN/ALQ-184 ECM pod. Converted into a QF-4G, the aircraft was expended in a missile test in June 2001.

11
F-4G-43-MC 69-7211 of the 81st TFS/4404th CW(P), Dhahran AB, Saudi Arabia, February 1992

The 81st TFS (re-named 81st FS after March 1992) sent F-4G detachments to Dhahran and to the 7440th CW(P) at Incirlik AB until early 1993, when its aircraft were gradually transferred to the re-activated 561st FS at Nellis AFB. 69-7211, with F-117A silhouettes on both intakes, displays 27 'Spook' mission markings on its port vari-ramp. Most of the F-4Gs' mission scores were applied for public display purposes after *Desert Storm*. Another ex-RAAF F-4E, this aircraft was taken into Tracor Flight Systems Inc's QF-4G drone conversion programme in December 1996 and expended in a missile test in November 2002.

12
F-4G-42-MC 69-0298 of the 190th FS/124th FG (Idaho ANG) assigned to the 7440th CW(P), Incirlik AB, December 1995

The non-standard four-figure serial presentation on the fin of this aircraft was used because the 190th FS also had 69-7298 on strength at this time. Both jets came in a batch of 36 aircraft supplied by the 35th and 52nd FWs from the summer of 1991 onwards. This example retained its 'weaselmouth' markings until placed in storage at AMARC in April 1996. Idaho's *Weasels*, coded 'WW' from 1994, shared SEAD CAP responsibilities during OSW patrols over Iraq with the 561st FS. A HARM attack on an AAA

radar site on 29 June 1993 is recorded on the jet's port vari-ramp splitter plate. Converted into a QF-4G, this aircraft was expended in a missile test over the Gulf of Mexico in May 1998.

13
F-4G-43-MC 69-7232 of the 561st FS/57th Wing, Dhahran AB, Saudi Arabia, January 1996

This F-4G, flown by Lt Col Randy Gelwix (then CO of the 81st TFS) and Maj Jim Uken, led the first flight of Coalition aircraft to enter Iraqi-controlled airspace on the opening night of *Desert Storm*. After its reactivation within the 57th FW in February 1993, the 561st FS resumed OSW patrols, and this aircraft, assigned to Lt Cols Mark Turberville and Jim Uken, led the last F-4G mission of the operation on 11 January 1996. Uken noted that it was 'the last US F-4 to exit hostile territory'. Wearing the Air Combat Command shield, it has the 57th Wing's chequered tailband incorporating the squadron's 'black knight helmet' insignia and the HARM symbols for eight missile site kills, earned with the 81st TFS during *Desert Storm* (Uken pointed out that 'the first three kills are actually from Lt Col Gelwix and me'). Below them on the port vari-ramp is a weasel cartoon and the famous *YGBSM!* motto. Crew names have been removed. Within two months of completing its final OSW mission, 69-7232 was in storage in AMARC awaiting conversion into a QF-4G later that same year.

14
F-4G-42-MC 69-0260 of the 23rd FS/7440th CW(P), Incirlik AB, Turkey, early 1991

The 23rd TFS deployed its F-16C/F-4G teams to Incirlik from December 1990 to March 1991, crews supporting strikes by 7440th CW(P) aircraft. This F-4G had 15 'spook' symbols marked up when it was assigned to the 81st FS. Two 23rd TFS F-4Gs had SA-2 director-transporter vehicle silhouettes applied to their port vari-ramps, while 69-0285 added an IrAF Il-76 transport to its mission score. Sent to AMARC in March 1996, this aircraft was destroyed by a missile in September 2002.

15
F-4G-42-MC 69-0278 of the 561st FS/57th Wing (4404th CW(P)), Dhahran AB, Saudi Arabia, January 1996

This F-4G, depicted during the last month of the 561st FS's F-4G OSW operations, displays four unusually large, confirmed *Desert Storm* missile site kill markings and a 'Spook' that is a reminder of the F-4's long USAF career. Its 'Black Knights' insignia also appears on the intake and within the 57th Wing's chequered tailband. The ECM pods in use were basically the same ones carried during *Desert Storm*. 69-0278 was sent to AMARC in February 1996, converted into a QF-4G shortly thereafter and destroyed in a missile test in May 2005.

16
F-4G-42-MC 69-0265 of the 561st TFS/35th TFW(P), Shaikh Isa AB, Bahrain, January 1991

Typical of the toned-down camouflage worn by both F-4G squadrons at Shaikh Isa AB for *Desert Storm*, this aircraft lacks any squadron identification markings. The TAC shield on the tail was usually overpainted too. Another anomaly was the painting of the entire sensor/gun housing under the nose in Gunship Gray. 69-0265 joined the QF-4G conversion line at Mojave, in California, in September 1997 following 15 months in storage at AMARC. It was destroyed in a missile test in March 1999.

17

F-4G-45-MC 69-7579 of the 561st FS/57th Wing (4404th CW(P)), Dhahran AB, Saudi Arabia, January 1996

Amongst the last F-4Gs to undertake OSW missions, 69-7579 had its port vari-ramp adorned with yet another version of a *'Wild Weasel'* and four SAM kills. The jet made its first flight on 10 March 1971 as an F-4E and its last on 18 August 1999 as a QF-4G, when it was destroyed in a missile test. Whilst based at Dhahran, the aircraft's task was the protection of Coalition reconnaissance flights from SAMs and AAA, the F-4G working closely with F-15C Eagles in the enforcement of the no-fly zone over southern Iraq.

18

F-4G-44-MC 69-7294 of the 90th TFS/3rd TFW, Clark AB, Philippines, 1991

In its former guise as an F-4E, this was the 4000th Phantom II to be delivered (in February 1971) and it was converted to F-4G configuration in December 1989. The 90th TFS flew 'sharkmouthed' F-4Es and 12 F-4Gs, received in 1979 and used until May 1991. Most of the F-4Gs then moved to the 35th and 52nd TFWs, although this aircraft was passed on to the 190th FS before eventual conversion into a QF-4G in 1997 and destruction in a missile test in November 1998.

19

F-4G-42-MC 69-0272 of 190th FS/124th FG (7440th CW(P)), Incirlik AB, Turkey, December 1995

Wearing a 'lo-viz' Idaho ANG tailband in Light Ghost Gray FS 26118 and Medium Gray FS 26270, this F-4G has extravagant 'weasel mouth' artwork to distinguish it from the squadron's 'sharkmouthed' F-4Es. The 124th FG ran the last ANG Phantom Replacement Training Unit, preparing both F-4G and RF-4C crews until the last examples of the photo-reconnaissance Phantom IIs were removed at the end of 1993, allowing the unit to concentrate on the SEAD role. During OSW, Idaho F-4Gs carried the AN/ALQ-184(V)1, 3 or 5 'long' ECM pods. After being sent to AMARC in April 1996, 69-0272 was converted into a QF-4G and expended in a missile test in February 2002.

20

F-4G-42-MC 69-0293 of the 81st TFS/52nd TFW, Dhahran AB, Saudi Arabia, February 1992

Credited with six confirmed SAM site kills, this *Wild Weasel* had its squadron markings removed for *Desert Storm* and re-instated (as seen here) on return to Spangdahlem and for subsequent OSW deployments. It was later transferred to Nellis AFB with the 57th FW, and ended its days as a range target at the Nevada base. Kill markings or other artwork were often removed from F-4Gs upon their re-assignment to Nellis AFB.

21

F-4G-42-MC 69-0251 of the 37th TFW, George AFB, California, early 1989

This F-4G became the 35th TFW commander's 'colour jet', and its markings were revised several times to display the Wing's title and its various squadron colours. These changed again when the aircraft flew with the 561st FS Detachment to the 4404th CW(P) at Dhahran, where it was eventually marked with five SAM radar kills, some achieved during *Desert Storm*. The four-HARM loadout depicted here

was used for shorter-ranging *Desert Storm* missions. Amongst the first F-4Gs sent to AMARC, in April 1992, 69-0251 was converted into a QF-4G in 1998 and expended in a missile test in July 2001.

22

F-4G-42-MC 69-0273 of the 561st TFS/35th TFW, George AFB, California, August 1990

Seen here with a 'standard' combat load of two AIM-7F Sparrows, two AGM-88B HARMs, a 600-gallon Royal Jet centreline tank, two wing tanks and an AN/ALQ-184 ECM pod, this 561st TFS F-4G is ready for the long transit flight to Bahrain for Operation *Desert Shield* and what Lt Gen 'Chuck' Horner called the 'aerial ballet' of combat operations. After its final service with the Idaho ANG, 69-0273 spent a year in storage before QF-4G conversion in January 1997.

23

F-4G-44-MC 69-7556 of the 81st TFS/52nd TFW, Shaikh Isa AB, Bahrain, March 1991

One of the high scorers during *Desert Storm,* this aircraft was credited with six SAM sites and radars destroyed, although these successes were not recorded on its vari-ramp when the jet returned to Spangdahlem on 5 April 1991. Some 81st TFS aircraft, like 69-7556, retained their squadron tail bands whilst in-theatre, but all had unit insignia deleted. The *Desert Shield* detachment drew aircraft and personnel from all the 52nd TFW squadrons to become a 24-aircraft Unit Equipped squadron at Shaikh Isa by 1 January 1991, when they were all assigned to 81st TFS control. 69-7556 remained in service at Nellis AFB until it entered storage in 1996. Converted into a QF-4G two years later, the jet was lost over the Gulf of Mexico in April 1999 during a missile test.

24

F-4G-43-MC 69-7235 of Detachment 5 of the 4485th TES, Tactical Air Warfare Centre, Eglin AFB, Florida, 1987

This aircraft was one of three Phantom IIs assigned to Detachment 5 from July 1987 for the development of F-4G weapons and avionics and the evolution of SEAD tactics for implementation by George's 562nd TFTS in its training syllabuses. The detachment was staffed by some of the most experienced crews in the EW and SEAD areas. In its previous life as an F-4E, this Phantom II had downed a MiG-21 on 15 August 1972 over North Vietnam whilst being flown by Capts Fred Sheffler and Mark Massen of the 336th TFS/8th TFW. Ending its USAF service with the 561st TFS, the aircraft spent six months at AMARC prior to being converted into a QF-4G in May 1996. It was shot down by an F-16 in a missile test over the Gulf Test Range Complex off the west coast of Florida in May 1998.

INDEX

References to images are in **bold**.